The Habsburg
Empire in
European Affairs,
1814-1918

The Habsburg Empire in European Affairs, 1814-1918

by Barbara Jelavich

ARCHON BOOKS 1975

Library of Congress Cataloging in Publication Data

Jelavich, Barbara Brightfield.
    The Habsburg Empire in European Affairs, 1814-1918.

    Reprint of the ed. published by Rand McNally, Chi-
cago, in series: the Rand McNally European history series.
    Bibliography: p.
    1. Habsburg, House of. 2. Europe — Politics — 1815-
1871. 3. Europe — Politics — 1871-1918. I. Title.
DB80.J4   1974   327.436'04   74-16338
ISBN 0-208-01485-3

Editor's Preface

It used to be thought that the sole object of history was to discover and set forth the facts. When the *English Historical Review* was founded it recommended such a procedure, for through it one "can usually escape the risk of giving offense." While much of this tradition has remained active in the teaching and writing of history, it has led, in turn, to a sharp reaction against such timidity and narrowness. History became a branch of philosophy or of the social sciences, and scholarship was in danger of being displaced by the search for general laws that might govern the development of all mankind. There is a hunger for history abroad in the land, but many of those who want to know about the past are rightly dissatisfied with arid narrations of fact (and turn to the historical novel instead), while others are bewildered by abstruse generalizations that seem to ignore the particular for the universal.

The books in the Rand McNally European History Series do not place themselves in either of these traditions. Instead, they recognize both the importance of accurate and detailed scholarship and the obligation to place such scholarship within a meaningful historical setting. They do not shun general ideas and assumptions; they test them in the crucible of research. This combination is always exciting, because it penetrates historical development; and this development, in each of its stages, illuminates a new dimension of mankind. A prominent historian once wrote, "What man is, only history tells."

Here "what man is" is told by scholars who have researched and reflected upon a significant period of history. They have taken this opportunity to present their conclusions in a manner that will attract and stimulate those who long for a lively account of the past. All of the authors in this series are specialists presenting their original insights, making it possible for all those interested in history to partake of their work.

George L. Mosse, *advisory editor*
Rand McNally European History Series

Preface

This survey is designed to present the position of the Habsburg Monarchy in European affairs in the period from the Congress of Vienna until the dissolution of the monarchy following World War I. Because of the central position of the state on the European continent the empire played a major role in European diplomacy, particularly in the years between 1815 and 1848, the "Age of Metternich." Thereafter, internal controversy and the consolidation of central and southeastern Europe into national states resulted in the gradual weakening of the Habsburg ability to control and influence the course of European history. Emphasis has thus been placed in this account on the unique problems in international relations facing a state that was essentially conservative in political orientation and that was composed of eleven national groups in an age of liberal and national revolutions. The attempt has also been made to describe the general European background of each diplomatic crisis so that this book will be of use to those who do not have a previous close acquaintance with the main issues in international relations in this period.

In the following pages the spelling of proper names and geographic terms will usually follow common English usage. It is thus Aix-la-Chapelle, not Aachen; Laibach, not Ljubljana; and Francis Joseph, not Franz Joseph. Most first names have been anglicized, but exceptions have been made when another form is more familiar. The terms "Austria" and "the Austrian Empire" are used to refer to the entire monarchy until the Ausgleich of 1867; thereafter "Austria" is used only as the name for one part of the Dual Monarchy, with "Austria-Hungary" the designation for the state as a whole.

The manuscript of this book was read by Professor Enno E. Kraehe of the University of Virginia, Professor Paul W. Schroeder of the University of Illinois, and Professors Harry Young and Charles Jelavich of Indiana University. I am extremely grateful for their comments and suggestions and for their appreciation of the problems to be faced in the study of Habsburg foreign policy. Professor Norman J. G. Pounds of Indiana University was kind enough to prepare the map of 1815. I also wish to express my appreciation to the members of my colloquium in East European History in the summer of 1968, my seminar in the fall of 1968, with whom most of this manuscript was discussed, and to Mark and Peter Jelavich. The publication of this account was aided immensely by the expert editorial assistance of Miss Phyllis Burke.

                                        Barbara Jelavich
January, 1969
Bloomington, Indiana

Contents

Introduction

In the century from 1814 to 1914 five great powers—Britain, France, Prussia (Germany after 1870), Russia and the Habsburg Empire—dominated European affairs and by extension those of most of the world. After 1860 Italy joined this number. Although these states shared many attributes, they differed in their relative success in internal affairs and in international relations. Each was unique in its patterns of life; each possessed its own strengths and its own weaknesses.

As the nineteenth century progressed, it became increasingly apparent that in both foreign and domestic policy the advantages lay with those nations whose inner structures most closely conformed with the new economic and social patterns evolving in Europe. Certainly the model state in this period was Britain, the first of the powers to exploit effectively the technological advances and to develop a powerful industrial society. In internal politics control of the government was shifted, without revolution or intensive internal strife, from the old landowning aristocracy to the middle classes, whose strength lay in the new economic system. Internal stability and economic power gave Britain the resources and background for a successful foreign policy. Exploiting her island position, which eliminated the necessity of maintaining a costly army, she concentrated on the development of those lines of policy that best suited her resources and national character. The building of predominant naval power and the assembling of the world's mightiest empire became her chief tasks.

Concurrent with this emphasis on her world position, Britain, where possible, limited her European commitments to those actions that were needed for the preservation of the balance of power on the continent. Associated with the emphasis on imperial and commercial interests was the special position in British foreign policy of the Ottoman Empire and the importance at this time of the Eastern Question. Britain in the nineteenth century was also

1

favored with a succession of remarkably able statesmen and diplomats who knew well how to make use of Britain's advantages and to avoid involvement in affairs that could bring them no concrete gains.

France also, even with her frequent internal crises and the great military defeats of 1814, 1815 and 1870, played a leading and generally successful part in European international relations. Like Britain, she too participated in the great economic advances of the time, although with a different emphasis. A relatively strong economic position, particularly in finance, together with basic social stability in spite of much surface revolutionary activity, gave her the resources for an active foreign policy and the maintenance of a respected army. In addition, France enjoyed in international affairs an advantage not shared by other powers. Despite the ultimate failure of the French revolutionary leaders and Napoleon to impose upon Europe the political patterns they represented, France did retain her reputation as the center for the propagation of liberalism and nationalism, the two dominant political ideas of the century. Although the belief that Paris was the center of revolutionary conspiracy complicated French relations with extremely conservative powers, tsarist Russia in particular, it did mean that the most progressive and active of Europe's young leaders turned to France for guidance and inspiration. It was a weapon that the French could utilize in their own national interest.

Throughout the century the most rapid rise in national power and prestige was shown by Prussia and, after the unification, by the new German Empire. The Germans, like the British, underwent the same fundamental shift to an industrial economy, although later in the century. The development of great manufacturing complexes together with the national spirit engendered by the unification made Germany by the turn of the century the most formidable military power of the time. Like Britain and France, Prussia and then Germany went through a process of political evolution toward the establishment of constitutional government. Here, however, national and socialist tendencies played a more active role in political life than they did in the island kingdom.

To the east the largest of the European great powers—Russia—stood distinctly behind these three in both politics and economics. The government remained autocratic in form until 1905; industrial development commenced late in the century and did not attain levels comparable to those of the Western states. Nevertheless, throughout this period Russia played constantly a leading role in international relations and enjoyed a reputation for military strength that was probably not consistent with reality. Her great natural advantages lay in her geographic position on the edge of the areas of major tension, her enormous land mass, which made invasion frightful for an outside power to contemplate, and her large population of potential soldiers.

As has been indicated, all four of these nations held a dominating position in world affairs in the nineteenth century. In addition, each achieved a major accretion of national territory, and, with the possible exception of Russia, each was able to guarantee her citizens throughout the century an ever-rising standard of living. The growth in the power and the prestige of these states can best be indicated by a comparison of a world, not a European, map of 1815 with a world map of 1914. Within that period these nations acquired vast stretches of territory, and millions of subject people were brought under their control.

The fifth nation, the Habsburg Empire, followed an entirely different path: unlike its companions on the European scene its way led downward—toward a steady diminution of power in international relations and to eventual political disintegration. As a state in a world of competing great powers, the Habsburg Empire thus emerges as a loser in history. The question naturally arises of why this development occurred. Certainly in economic progress the empire compared favorably with the surrounding states. In fact, the economic advantages of the union of the lands centered on the Danube was one of the cohesive forces of the state. In political development also the evolution within the country, although very slow, kept pace with that of the neighboring lands, particularly those to the south and east. The basis of the Habsburg weakness thus must be sought not in the events of the historical period with which we are dealing but in the nature of the state itself, its geographic position and its inability to adopt successfully the accepted political patterns of its age.

In the nineteenth century the Habsburg Empire was radically different from the other great powers in two attributes: first, it lacked a real national base, and, second, in most instances the central government had been unable to destroy the ability of the historical divisions of their lands to claim the prime loyalty of their inhabitants.

In contrast, the four other powers by the end of the nineteenth century had achieved internal consolidation and they were national states. Although France, Britain, Germany and Russia did control large numbers of alien people, each state was clearly the possession of one national group, with one cultural pattern and language. The rivalry of internal political divisions with the central government had in each case been effectively broken. The majority of the population looked upon themselves first as members of the wider national group. This domestic cohesion, which was an important attribute of all the national states of the age, allowed most of them to adopt centralized rather than federal forms of administration. In war and diplomacy this type of political organization was to prove far more effective than any decentralized or supranational combination.

The reasons the Habsburg Empire came to contrast so fundamentally with the other European great powers are best found in an examination of the historical development of the state and the national composition of its territories. The history of the empire is centered around the rise of the Habsburg dynasty. Like the other great royal families of Europe, whose former possessions form the basis of the national states, it grew in power and influence through the absorption of smaller and weaker political units. Unlike the acquisitions of other dynasties, the Habsburg territories were of widely varying national composition. The original family lands lay in southwest Germany and in Switzerland. In the fourteenth century, through marriage alliances and victories in war and diplomacy, the core lands of the empire, those roughly equivalent to present-day Austria, were added. These territories were German in language and culture. After 1273 the Habsburg rulers, with only a few exceptions, regularly held the title of Holy Roman Emperor. Although this position carried but little political power, it did give the Habsburg rulers the first rank among the German princes. The most important permanent shift in the national basis of the empire occurred when the kingdoms of Bohemia (1526), Croatia (1527) and Hungary (1527) passed under Habsburg control. Further non-German lands were obtained in the course of the long wars that the empire waged with both the Ottoman Empire and France. In 1742 the predominantly German province of Silesia was lost to Prussia. At the end of the eighteenth century Polish territories were acquired when Austria participated with Prussia and Russia in the partition of that state. Through this process the German component of the empire was reduced to a minority of the entire population.

During the major part of the history of the state these various lands were held together by the fact that they were the possessions of the dynasty. Provincial institutions were in general preserved. Few attempts were made to centralize the administration or to destroy the political power of the local nobility except where this group actively combatted Habsburg overlordship. In 1713, for the first time, Charles VI in the Pragmatic Sanction declared his lands the indivisible possessions of the head of the Habsburg dynasty. It was not until 1804 that this complex of territories received a title—the Austrian Empire. As long as the Habsburg provinces retained their historic individuality and remained under traditional local leadership, the question of the nationality of the ruling groups of the state was not the burning issue it was later to become. The Habsburgs were a German family. German was to become the main language of culture and administration. Because of the predominance of Germans in the aristocracy, the cities and the church, the entire empire acquired in time a general appearance that, although typically Habsburg in detail, was very similar to that of the central European lands in general. However, as in all of Europe, French became the language of diplomacy and often the preferred means of communication among the aristocracy; Latin was the official language of Hungary. The empire was not, nor did it ever become, a German state. It was rather a complex of nations associated together in an intricate relationship, in which a German dynasty ruled and a German aristocracy and urban middle-class enjoyed a special position. Undoubtedly the national diversity and the decentralization of the state contributed to a weakening of the Habsburg position in foreign affairs. Britain and France consistently showed a superior effectiveness. However, as long as the entire central European area remained in a similar condition, the empire could compete successfully in international affairs.

In the eighteenth century new political concepts, based on the principles of the Enlightenment, gained in acceptance even among the monarchs of Europe. Most significant for the Habsburg Empire was the shift from the idea of the autocrat to the concept of the ruler as the first servant of his people, and the change from the divine-right foundation for political power to that of the sovereignty of the people. At this time attempts were made to put these concepts into practice in eastern Europe by a succession of rulers known as the Enlightened Despots. In the Habsburg Empire Joseph II's tragic career was characterized by his efforts to reform his government along these lines and to introduce a more logical and rational system of administration into his domains. His policies of centralization were strongly opposed in the historic divisions of the empire; the use of German as the language of administration was naturally disliked by the non-German peoples. The failure of these reforms did not encourage Joseph's successors to follow in similar paths. The French Revolution, however, gave added impetus to the new political ideals. In the period of this movement and of the rule of Napoleon not only the idea of constitutional government but also that of the national state received wide acceptance. After 1815, even though the French armies were defeated, the principles of liberalism and nationalism as revolutionary forces remained.

In international relations these concepts were to continue to have a dominating influence throughout the century. Four of the great powers, as we have seen, were already national states; the acceptance of the national idea merely strengthened their positions. These same states could also gradually adopt liberal principles in internal affairs without endangering the cohesion of their territories. In contrast, as will be shown, the Habsburg Empire, because of its complex multinational structure, could not so easily accept other forms of government, although certainly the attempt was made. The period between 1848 and 1914 is filled with constitutional experimentation aimed at discovering a type of government suitable to the situation. A solution was never found.

Because of the ultimate determining effect of the nationality problem upon the fate of the monarchy a brief description should be given of its peoples. The empire was composed chiefly of eleven national groups: Croats, Czechs, Germans, Italians, Magyars, Poles, Rumanians, Ruthenians (Ukrainians), Serbs, Slovaks and Slovenes. Two of these, the Germans and the Magyars, comprising together about half the population, enjoyed distinct social and political advantages. Next, the Czechs, Poles, Croats and Italians occupied a middle position. Below them lay the predominantly peasant peoples—the Serbs, Slovenes, Slovaks, Rumanians and Ruthenians. It will be noted that of these peoples only the Croats, Czechs, Magyars, Slovenes and Slovaks were contained within the boundaries of the empire. In contrast, the Germans, Italians, Poles, Serbs, Rumanians and Ruthenians could look outward to other states inhabited by co-nationals. With the rise of the Yugoslav movement in the late nineteenth century the Croats and Slovenes as well as the Serbs were attracted to the in-

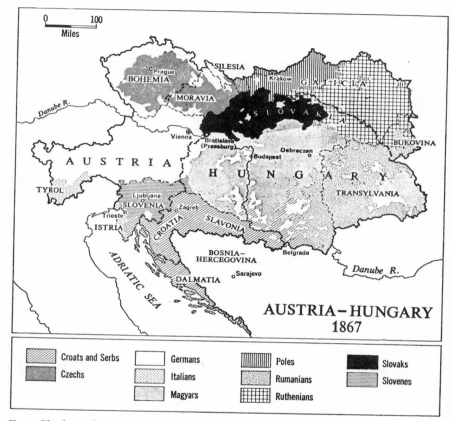

Croats and Serbs   Germans   Poles   Slovaks
Czechs   Italians   Rumanians   Slovenes
Magyars   Ruthenians

AUSTRIA–HUNGARY
1867

From Charles and Barbara Jelavich, *The Habsburg Monarchy: Toward a Multinational Empire or National States* (New York: Rinehart & Company, 1959), p. 2. Cartography by Vincent Kotschar.

dependent state of Serbia. The Habsburg government thus not only had to deal with the conflict of groups within its boundaries, it had to resist the attraction that other nations might exert upon its citizens.

Although for the most part the national groups did live clustered together in distinct geographical sections of the country, the historical territorial divisions only generally coincided with this ethnic distribution. Moreover, within these areas certain national groups, those with a strong aristocracy, tended to dominate over a peasant population of another nationality. Thus in Galicia Polish nobles held control over Ruthenian and Polish peasants; in Transylvania a Magyar minority had more political power than either the Rumanian peasantry or the Germans of the towns.

The natural disintegrating forces that were bound to be at work within a multinational empire in an age of nationalism were felt more strongly as the nineteenth century advanced. The Habsburg rulers, nevertheless, had important and effective weapons with which they could maintain the unity of their lands. Certainly in the preceding centuries the empire had played a great role in European history. From the fifteenth to the eighteenth century the union of its lands had been needed to provide an effective barrier against the Ottoman Empire. When that power lost its aggressive character and began its long retreat from Europe, the Austrian state was still regarded by most powers as a European necessity because of the part it took in maintaining the European balance of power. In addition, despite its frequent internal crises, the empire until its downfall in 1918 did continue to command the loyalties of most of its people. The traditional institutions of attraction were the Habsburg dynasty, a symbol around which all could unite, the bureaucracy, which provided good administration, and the army, in which all of the peoples served together. The Catholic church, representing the faith of approximately 80 per cent of the population, also proved a support of the empire and the Habsburg dynasty.

Nevertheless, despite these cohesive forces the Habsburg government, with this internal structure, had to deal with issues in foreign policy that were unique. No other great power throughout the century under study faced a similar situation. The British had their Irish problem and the Russians had a Polish question, but in neither case did the national issue involve the existence and integrity of the great power. In contrast, the Habsburg government was forced to meet the challenge of four major national movements—the German, the Italian, the Magyar and the Serb (Yugoslav)— and three others of lesser immediate danger—the Rumanian, the Czech and the Polish. The complete victory of the Magyar, the Czech or the Yugoslav national idea meant the dissolution of the empire; the triumph of the others signified a great weakening of the power of the state. Because of this situation the internal and international affairs of the empire intertwine to a far greater degree than is true of any other European great power. Thus a study of Habsburg foreign relations must always be closely related to the progress of domestic affairs, particularly the national question.

In addition to these issues the Habsburg diplomats had to meet a second set of problems, which arose largely from the geographic position of the country. In 1814 the center of Europe, from the North Sea through the Italian peninsula, was divided into small political units. On the wings stood the two great powers, France and Russia. Throughout the century the Habsburg Empire had to combat the natural tendency of these two states to expand into the center. French pressure was directed toward Italy and the Rhine, Russian toward the Polish lands and into the Balkans. The empire also had to face Prussia's constant attempts within the German area to gain supremacy at least north of the river Main. As will be seen, Russia, Prussia and France were all able to use the national weapon to gain victories against the Habsburg Empire.

The following account will be divided into three sections, each representing a division in the development of Habsburg foreign policy. In the first period, lasting from 1814 to 1848, the empire was able to maintain a strong position in central Europe. With the use of its army and possessed of the initiative and determination necessary to prevent changes in the areas under its control, the Habsburg government retained the advantages gained at the Congress of Vienna. The second period, from 1848 to 1870, marks the victory of the national movements in Rumania, Italy and Germany and, within the empire, the acquisition by the Magyars of a predominating position through the *Ausgleich*, or Compromise, of 1867. In the last section, dealing with the years from 1870 to 1918, the decline in power and the eventual dissolution of the monarchy is discussed. During this time Habsburg foreign policy was, of necessity, primarily concerned with Balkan problems and was strongly influenced by both German and Magyar interests.

Part I

The Age of Metternich: 1814–1848

Chapter 1

The Congress of Vienna

In September 1814 the rulers of Europe and their chief ministers met in Vienna to attempt to settle the problems resulting from twenty-five years of virtually constant war and revolutionary upheaval. The host nation was represented by Emperor Francis and his chief minister, Prince Clemens von Metternich, one of the most respected statesmen of Europe and the "diplomatic conqueror" of Napoleon. The British government sent its foreign secretary, Viscount Castlereagh, and the hero of the Spanish war, the Duke of Wellington. The handsome and erratic Tsar Alexander I, assisted by his numerous non-Russian advisers, Capodistrias, Nesselrode, Stein and Czartoryski, was usually closely supported by the Prussian king, Frederick William III, and his ministers, Hardenberg and Humboldt. The interests of defeated France were defended with skill and craft by Talleyrand.

For the Habsburg Empire the preceding quarter-century had been a period of continual military disaster. The wars against the armies of the French Revolution and Napoleon had led to repeated losses of territory and to a sharp decline of Austrian power. The imperial family had seen the epoch commence with the execution of Marie Antoinette, the sister of Emperor Leopold, and end with the marriage to Napoleon of Marie Louise, the daughter of Emperor Francis. Like all of the great powers of Europe, Austria sought at the conference a settlement that would offer security against a revival of another similar period of war and revolution. Austrian finances were in a desperate condition; the land needed peace to recover from the long wars and the ravages of foreign invasion. The Austrian government, again like that of the other powers, saw its safety best secured by the reestablishment of the international equilibrium, by a restoration of the former dynasties and states to their previous positions and by an emphasis on the principles of order and legitimacy. The peace at Vienna was made by the four victor states, Austria, Prussia, Russia and Britain, with the participation of France. There was no disagreement among them on the aims and concepts that should form the basis of the future peace. No state was ready to accept radical innovations in international relations or to attempt experimentation with new forms.

The relaxation felt by all of Europe's leaders is perhaps best shown by the general atmosphere of the conference, which lasted over nine months. Although the real decisions were made by consultation among the great powers, all of the smaller states sent their rulers and ministers. To entertain this crowd of dignitaries the Austrian government and the great aristocratic families provided a succession of entertainments—balls, theater presentations, excursions, receptions, etc.—which the state could ill afford. These distractions delayed the proceedings but provided an atmosphere in which a peace of reconciliation could be made by statesmen who were well acquainted with one another and who had the leisure to consider the main problems.

The congress was not concerned with the question of defeated France. The first peace of Paris of May 1814 had settled the terms of the French surrender. At this time, in a generous settlement, France had agreed to accept the boundaries of 1792. Napoleon was sent to the island of Elba; Louis XVIII returned as king of France. No attempt was made to overturn the chief administrative reforms of the Napoleonic period; Louis XVIII granted a modified constitution, the Charter. After the congress had lasted approximately six months, and when the major work had been completed, it was interrupted by Napoleon's return to France and the period of the Hundred Days. The second peace of Paris, following Napoleon's defeat, imposed more stringent terms. An indemnity was leveled and an army of occupation was to remain in France until full payment was made. France was returned to the boundaries of 1790. This time Napoleon was exiled to the remote island of St. Helena.

In the meetings at the congress the chief controversy that arose concerned the fate of Poland and of Saxony. At the end of the war it was apparent that with the destruction of French military might Russia emerged as the strongest power on the continent. In the last stages of the war and throughout the peace negotiations Frederick William III cooperated closely with Alexander I. This combination, with Russia as the dominating partner, was looked upon with apprehension by both Metternich and Castlereagh. Naturally British and Austrian interests would be ill served should Russia replace France as the power that threatened to secure hegemony in Europe. Moreover, the character and words of Alexander I aroused great distrust. It was never quite clear what he wanted or how far he would go toward seeking to secure predominant Russian power in Europe.

Certainly the Russian and Prussian desires for territorial increases seemed dangerous. Alexander now proposed that the territories of Napoleon's Duchy of Warsaw, which had been formed from the Austrian and Prussian shares in the partition of Poland, be made into a separate Polish nation. This state, Congress Poland, was to be autonomous, with its own administration, but it was to be joined to Russia through the person of the tsar. It was to receive also a constitutional form of government. Prussia, in return for her Polish lands, was to be compensated with the annexation of the kingdom of Saxony; Austria would receive lands in Italy and the former Illyrian Provinces.

Obviously these changes would be of tremendous strategic significance. To the other powers the establishment of a Polish state joined to Russia in any manner whatsoever was the equivalent of a Russian annexation. This advance of Russian control would bring the borders of that state within 175 miles of Vienna. Russian possession of Cracow would deliver into her hands the key to the northern entrance of the Moravian Gate, the easy passage through the Carpathians to the heart of the Austrian empire. The Prussian acquisition of Saxony would greatly increase the power and influence of Prussia within the German area and extend the length of the Austro-Prussian common border.

Russian and Prussian insistence on these terms produced a real crisis. In January 1815 Austria and Britain joined with France in a treaty, which was also adhered to by some of the German states,

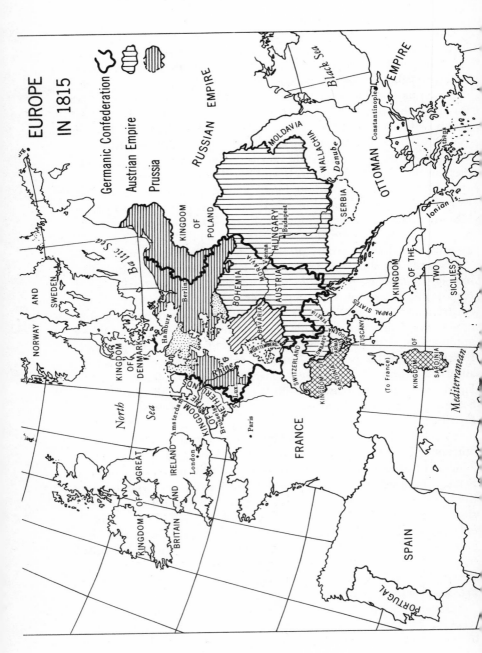

Cartography by Norman J. G. Pounds.

designed to oppose the Russian and Prussian proposals. Faced with a new coalition and unwilling to accept a further war, Alexander I retreated. He did indeed receive the right to establish a Polish state, but it was reduced to two-thirds of the size he desired. Austria received back Polish territories in Galicia; Prussia retained Posen, Thorn and Danzig. Cracow was made a free city. Prussia took only about half of Saxony's territory and instead was given more land in the Rhineland. With this conflict settled the powers agreed with less friction to the other rearrangements of the map of Europe.

In the settlement of general European questions Austrian interests were involved more deeply in assuring her predominant position in the Italian peninsula and among the German states than in acquiring additional territory. The Habsburg government was, nevertheless, interested in consolidating and rounding off its possessions and in maintaining its position on the Adriatic. Thus in order to achieve a better organization of the Austrian lands, Metternich willingly gave up control of Belgium and of Rhenish territories, which had been part of the ancient possessions of the house of Habsburg. The Belgian lands were joined with the kingdom of Holland; the others were acquired principally by Prussia. The aim of both of these moves was to establish a stronger barrier against French expansion toward the Rhine or the Low Countries. In return Austria obtained Istria, Dalmatia and Venetia. She also regained the Tyrol and Galicia, and she kept the Salzburg area, which had been taken previously from Bavaria, who in turn was indemnified with other territories in Germany.

In the reorganization of the German states the Habsburg Empire was able to secure a settlement in accordance with its interests and wishes. Although little heed was paid to the liberal and national currents that remained from the previous period, the conditions prevalent before the French Revolution were not restored. In 1806 Emperor Francis had abandoned the title of Holy Roman Emperor; the position was not reestablished. In addition, the old Germany of over 300 political subdivisions remained buried forever. Instead, the area was now composed of thirty-nine political units, of which four were free cities. All were joined in a very loose union, the Germanic Confederation, which also included outside powers. Austria and Prussia, the strongest members of this organization, were represented only for the part of their domains that had been included in the defunct Holy Roman Empire. The Austrian lands of Dalmatia, Istria,

Lombardy-Venetia, Bukovina, Transylvania, Croatia-Slavonia and the Hungarian territories, and the Prussian districts of Pomerania, Posen, and east and west Prussia thus lay outside of the confederation. In addition, three non-German rulers participated—the king of England as ruler of Hanover (until 1837), the king of Denmark for Holstein and the king of Holland for Luxemburg.

The main organ of the confederation was the *Bundestag* (Federal Diet), which met in the free city of Frankfurt. It was composed of the delegates sent by the member states and was thus a kind of congress of ambassadors. Austria held the position of permanent president. Despite the fact that the bonds of this union were very weak, the confederation did have certain powers. It could send and receive foreign representatives, and it could make war and conclude treaties under certain circumstances. With all its faults it marked one step toward a possible consolidation of the German lands. Whether or not it would evolve in this direction depended largely on the course of future events and, in particular, on the attitude of Austria, who through this organization gained the leading position among the German states.

Habsburg vital interests were involved equally in the Italian settlement. Here the Austrian government gained conditions that assured its supremacy in the peninsula. As has been mentioned previously, the empire acquired the province of Venetia, which it joined to Lombardy, which had been held since 1714, to form the Kingdom of Lombardy-Venetia. In the south the Kingdom of the Two Sicilies again received a Bourbon ruler, Ferdinand I. The Papal States were restored to the possession of the pope. The two provinces of Tuscany and Modena went back to their former rulers, who were both members of the Habsburg family. Marie Louise, no longer empress of France, was consoled with the rule of Parma for her lifetime. The only state that could be expected to represent purely Italian interests and that had a native dynasty was Piedmont-Sardinia under the house of Savoy. It was now strengthened through the acquisition of Genoa.

Thus the Habsburg position was most favorable. Austria held territory in the north in her own right. The other states were in the hands of rulers who were either Habsburgs or whose interests were closely bound to those of Vienna. The king of Piedmont, Victor Emmanuel I, was extremely conservative and not likely to lead a national movement. Metternich had hoped to form an Italian league, which would play the same role in the peninsula that the Germanic Confederation did in Germany. The opposition of the pope as well as of Piedmont and Tuscany put an end to that idea.

To protect the highly advantageous Vienna settlement Austria joined in two general alliances. The first, the Holy Alliance, was the creation of Alexander I and the product of the spirit of religious exaltation and mysticism which was instilled within him during the Napoleonic invasion of 1812. The agreement consisted of little more than the declaration of the signatories that they would "both in the administration of their respective states and in their political relations" with each other base their actions on "the precepts of religion, namely, the rules of Justice, Christian Charity and Peace."[1] This pact was the subject of much derision at the time; Metternich referred to it as a "loud-sounding nothing."[2] To humor the tsar most of the European rulers signed it. Only the king of England, the sultan and the pope refused. As a diplomatic instrument the Holy Alliance never achieved a position of significance in international affairs. However, in the future the name was used to designate the close association established, particularly after 1820, among its three original signatories, Russia, Prussia and Austria. The term will be used henceforth to refer to this combination. The phrase "the alliance of the three northern courts" was also used at the time to refer to this diplomatic alignment.

The Quadruple Alliance of November 1815 was a far more practical agreement. At this time the four victorious allies renewed the Treaty of Chaumont of 1814 and agreed to remain associated to protect the new settlement and to prevent the revival of French aggressive action. The pact also contained the provision that the signatories would

> renew their meetings at fixed periods . . . for the purpose of consulting upon their common interests, and for the consideration of measures which at each of those periods shall be considered the most salutary for the repose and prosperity of Nations and for the maintenance of the peace of Europe.[3]

---

[1] W. P. Cresson, *The Holy Alliance* (New York: Oxford University Press, 1922), p. 31.

[2] Harold Nicolson, *The Congress of Vienna* (New York: Viking Press, 1961), p. 250.

[3] Sir Charles Webster, *The Foreign Policy of Castlereagh: 1815–1822* (New York: Bell, 1947), p. 55.

Under this stipulation four great congresses, at Aix-la-Chapelle, Troppau, Laibach and Verona, were held in the next years.

The settlement reached at Vienna was thus of great advantage to the Habsburg government. The former balance between the great powers had been reestablished, a fact that was of importance to Britain as well as Austria. "Legitimate" rulers now replaced those who had previously held their position through revolutionary activity. The territorial possessions of the monarchy had been consolidated and increased. Austrian influence reached out to the north through the Germanic Confederation and into Italy through the close Habsburg ties with the Italian states. With the achievement of this condition the Habsburg Empire became a satiated state. Henceforth its chief aim in international relations was the protection of the conditions of 1815 as they applied to its own territories and interests and to Europe as a whole.

Chapter 2

The Metternich System

As we have seen, the Austrian diplomat responsible for the successful conclusion to the peacemaking was the foreign minister, Clemens
von Metternich. Since this statesman was to occupy a predominating
position in European diplomacy for almost forty years and to give
his name to an era, it might be well to examine the career, character
and ideas of this representative of his age. Metternich was born in
Coblenz in May 1773 of a Rhenish noble family. His father entered
Austrian state service when Metternich was still young. After being
tutored at home, he studied at the universities in both Strasbourg
and Mainz. When the wars of the French Revolution forced his
family to leave the Rhineland, Metternich moved with them to
Vienna, where he entered the Austrian diplomatic corps. After serv-
ing in various lesser posts he was finally appointed to the most important position of the time, that of ambassador to France. In Paris
he came to know Napoleon well. His quick rise was assisted by his
keen intelligence, his elegant manners, his handsome appearance
and his adroit diplomatic tactics.

In October 1809 he became minister of foreign affairs. At this time
the Habsburg Empire was in a most unenviable position. Repeated
military defeats had demoralized the state; the constant wars had
exhausted its finances. Metternich thus entered his new post with

few assets. Obviously Austria could not afford to risk war. Metternich had only the traditional Habsburg means of negotiation and marriage to protect the interests of the state. His first major act involved the second method. Napoleon, now deeply concerned with founding a dynasty, still lacked the first prerequisite—a son. He therefore divorced his wife Josephine and with the assistance of Metternich arranged a marriage with Marie Louise, the daughter of Emperor Francis. Although this action linked the house of Habsburg with a man whose family lacked a true aristocratic background, the Austrian government could hope to gain concrete advantages from the union and to repair some of the damage of the past. In 1811 the birth of a son to Marie Louise further strengthened the relations between Paris and Vienna.

Meanwhile, however, Napoleon's fortunes were changing. The Treaty of Tilsit, negotiated in 1807 with Russia, was obviously not functioning as intended. By 1811 both France and Russia were preparing for war. Napoleon now turned for assistance to Austria and Prussia, powers supposedly under his control because of their past military disasters. In February 1812 France signed a treaty of alliance with Prussia. In March Austria in a similar agreement promised to provide 30,000 men for the coming Russian campaign, but with the provision that they would be under Habsburg command. At this time Metternich, although he expected a French victory, played both sides. He assured St. Petersburg secretly that the Austrian troops would not go into action against the Russians.

The crushing defeat of Napoleon in 1812 faced the European powers with a new military and diplomatic situation. The hitherto virtually invincible general had lost his main armies and a tremendous store of military supplies. He still, however, enjoyed a reputation for military genius, and he had been defeated only in Russia; he was in control of central Europe and France. After Napoleon's armies were forced out of Russia, Alexander I, against the advice of some of his generals, decided to carry the war into Europe and to seek the final overthrow of his adversary. In February 1813 he signed the Treaty of Kalisch with Prussia, which joined that state to this endeavor. Britain, at war with France in Spain and on the seas, naturally supported any military action against France. With this coalition of powers on one side and with Napoleon, still supported by some German states, on the other, Metternich was afraid to join the allies and to risk further Austrian defeats by French arms. The general situation was certainly not clear. Napoleon continued to win minor engagements and to show much of his old genius as a military commander. Therefore Metternich first tried to establish Austria in the role of armed mediator between the two sides. As Napoleon's position weakened, Austria gradually moved into the allied camp. Mediation failed when Napoleon consistently refused to accept a peace based on the "natural frontiers" of France—the Rhine, the Pyrenees and the Alps. In September 1813 Francis met with his fellow emperors, Alexander I and Frederick William III, at Teplitz. Here they agreed to fight until victory was achieved. In the future peace Austria and Prussia were to be restored to their frontiers of 1805 and the Napoleonic Confederation of the Rhine was to be dissolved. Thus, by the time of the great Battle of the Nations at Leipzig in October 1813, Austria was an active participant in the allied coalition against Napoleon. Of the rulers of the major states only King Frederick August of Saxony remained loyal to the French emperor. As a result of the victory at Leipzig Metternich received the title of prince.

Even after this stunning defeat Napoleon continued to refuse the allied terms for a mediated peace. Austria, despite her ties with the other powers, was not intent upon removing Napoleon as the French ruler. After all, an Austrian archduchess was empress of France; Napoleon's heir was Francis' grandson. However, continued French intransigeance compelled the resumption of the fighting. In March 1814 the four powers signed the Treaty of Chaumont, in which it was agreed that no state should make a separate peace and that France would be reduced to her frontiers of 1792. At the end of the month the allied forces, led by Alexander I with Frederick William III at his side, entered Paris. In the following month Napoleon was compelled to abdicate, and the restored Bourbon government accepted the first peace of Paris.

The first phase of Metternich's career as Habsburg foreign minister had been highly successful. While the fighting continued he had maneuvered between the conflicting forces until it was clear that the allies would be victorious. Afterward, at the Congress of Vienna, he had been able to avoid the danger both he and Castlereagh feared—that Russia through her obvious military superiority would upset the balance on the continent and establish conditions that would give her hegemony there. With the signature of the treaty of Vienna in June 1815 Metternich gained the settlement he desired, and one he

believed would be advantageous not only for his own country but
for all of the European states. Hereafter his entire career was devoted to the protection of the map of Europe of 1815 and the treaties
of Vienna.

In his prolific writing extending through his long years in office
Metternich left a record of his views on politics and international
relations. In most respects they were similar to those of the leading
statesmen of the day, and they were shared by the aristocratic ruling
circles who had been deeply frightened by the events of the revolutionary period. Napoleon in his years of victory had indeed introduced many progressive institutions and advanced principles of
government into Europe, but this action had been accomplished
through the instrumentality of the French armies and French rule.
Napoleonic government had also meant conscription, heavy taxation
and the constant threat of war. These negative aspects were those
most closely associated with the ideas of the French Revolution in
the minds of most contemporary statesmen, even among those who
had been sympathetic to many of the concepts of the Enlightenment.
The noble principles of the first phase of the French Revolution appeared to have led inevitably to a military dictatorship within France
and French hegemony in Europe. A strong degree of nostalgia was
thus felt for the prerevolutionary days; the desire to restore the old
order and to return to the classical balance of power in international
relations, which at least assured the relative safety of the large states,
existed everywhere.

The system Metternich now supported called for a restoration of
what he regarded as the natural state of affairs in Europe. Here five
great powers checked and balanced one another. The territorial distribution of Vienna, based on the principle of compensation, was
designed to maintain as far as possible an equal division of strength.
Metternich recognized that these states were different in their basic
natures. Britain was an insular empire; France and Russia were centralized monarchies. Between them lay Prussia, the Habsburg Empire and the German and Italian areas of smaller political units.
Ideally Metternich would have liked to have organized a German
and an Italian federation, both under Habsburg guidance. As we
have seen, he succeeded in establishing only one. Within Austria he
wished also to maintain a decentralized system of administration,
with much power left in the hands of the historical provinces. A
central Europe in which the principle of federation would dominate

would thus lie between the two centralized national states of France and Russia. In this scheme Prussia was assigned a distinct role in the German area. Metternich hoped to bring that state into a partnership with the aim of maintaining the settlement of Vienna and the political status quo among the states of the Germanic Confederation.

Closely associated with his conception of stability and balance in international relations were Metternich's conservative views on the internal organization of the state. The Austrian minister never felt any sympathy for revolutionary ideas; they remained entirely foreign to his views on political life. He saw political change only as a part of recurrent historical cycles in which periods of anarchy alternated with those of order. He believed that "the entire phenomenon of political and social desire for progress was only a temporary manifestation leading in the eternal cycle of things to the restoration of the old institutions governed by principles."[4] He felt that he had lived through a period of anarchy and that it was now "his fate to be the apostle of European social conservatism."[5] He was often very pessimistic about his role in politics. In 1828 he wrote: "My life coincides with an abominable period. I came into the world either too early or too late; at present I am good for nothing. . . . I am spending my life propping up mouldering buildings."[6]

Because Metternich believed in the close association of the internal regimes of the powers with the stability of the international order, he was at times, particularly after 1820, to approve the doctrine that the allied powers in concert had the right, perhaps even the duty, to interfere in the internal affairs of states whose governments were threatened by revolutionary activity. In practice Metternich was to support the application of this theory only when it clearly benefited Austrian interests. As will be seen, he usually wished to apply the principle when it was a question of Austrian interference in the affairs of the German and Italian states, but not when it involved the action of other states either within the Habsburg sphere or in other parts of Europe.

Of the great powers after the Congress of Vienna Metternich continued to regard Russia and her activities as the most dangerous.

---

[4] Heinrich von Srbik, in the section "The Champion of Historical Order," in Henry F. Schwarz (Ed.), *Metternich: Coachman of Europe—Statesman or Evil Genius*. (Boston: D. C. Heath and Company, 1962), pp. 18, 19.
[5] *Ibid.*, p. 19.
[6] Albert Sorel, in the section "Metternich the Man," *Ibid.*, p. 5.

France, the defeated power, was not in a position to act alone; Prussia also lacked the strength to launch an independent policy. Britain under the guidance of Castlereagh showed the same concern for the balance of power and conservative political principles as did Austria. Alexander I, in contrast, was an unsettling factor in European affairs. In his political beliefs he tended to alternate between liberal and conservative tendencies. He was, for instance, quite willing to accept liberal constitutional regimes if they were instituted by the ruler of a state. He made himself a constitutional monarch in Congress Poland. In Germany he was to become the defender of the German rulers who wished to grant liberal reforms against Austrian wishes. Within his own realms he remained, nevertheless, the complete autocrat.

The disturbing influence of Alexander's ideas was shown at the first of the general conferences held after Vienna—the Congress of Aix-la-Chapelle. Here the principal issue under discussion was the final settlement of the French question. Since the French government had paid its reparations, the occupying troops were withdrawn. France was now associated with the Quadruple Alliance, although she did not become a formal signatory to the treaty. The discussion of the issues dealing with France went smoothly and without disagreement among the powers. However, Alexander I used the occasion of the meeting to propose an extension of the Holy Alliance. He wished another agreement signed in which the powers would guarantee one another's territorial possessions and the political systems in effect within each state. This proposal, which would have allowed unlimited interference in the internal affairs of any power, was strongly opposed by both Metternich and Castlereagh. Both saw in it veiled attempts by Alexander I to increase his own control in Europe. Metternich at this time was not willing to recognize any general right of intervention. However, since he did not wish to antagonize a monarch who might prove a supporter of his own actions against revolutionary activity, he let Castlereagh take the lead in combatting Alexander's proposals. The British representative firmly refused to accept any extension of the British alliance commitments. The British government regarded its obligations under the treaties in existence as limited to the promise to cooperate with the other victor powers should France again become a menace to European security.

Nevertheless, despite subsequent minor disagreements among the powers, they did remain united in the years immediately after the Congress of Vienna. For Austria, the defender of the status quo, this situation was most favorable. Her relations with all of the great powers were good. She was joined to Prussia and Russia by a common interest in fighting revolutionary activity. All three countries had gained from the peace; none wished for the moment major changes in the map of Europe. France, the former menace to the European order, was now, and in fact would be for many years hence, in no position to act. Metternich had established close relations with Castlereagh. Although the British government would accept no further treaty obligations, the two diplomats shared the same views on European politics. Having thus obtained the maximum in territorial acquisitions and influence, and having established a favorable diplomatic alignment, Metternich after 1815 became a strong defender of the sanctity of international treaties and the maintenance of the territorial status quo established at Vienna. The Austrian government was to retain this attitude until 1870, when the last major sections of the Vienna settlement in central Europe were torn to shreds.

As the major supporter of the old order in both internal and international affairs, the Habsburg Empire was henceforth to become the principal target of attack for those who wished changes in Europe, especially in the German and Italian lands. Despite the defeat of the French armies, the political principles on which the revolution had been based still held wide currency. During the Napoleonic period a great national upsurge had occurred throughout Germany, and also in the Italian peninsula. After 1815 certain groups, with students and intellectuals prominent among them, were keenly aware of the disadvantages of the division of their people. In the post-Vienna days the great Romantic movement, which spread all over Europe but had its strongest influence in the German lands, strengthened these national feelings and added color and depth to an ideal. To all of those who opposed the order established by the Congress of Vienna, Metternich and Austria became hated symbols of oppression. It was from those who wished to establish political regimes based on the sovereignty of the people, or who sought national unification and freedom from Austrian domination, that Metternich was to receive the main challenge to his system. In the

1820s and 1830s, national and liberal revolts occurred in both Italy and Germany, and all went down to defeat. By 1848 the forces against the status quo had grown so strong that, at least for a short time, they were able to pull down the entire edifice so carefully fashioned and protected by the Austrian minister.

The Challenge in Germany

After the Congress of Vienna the first area in which Metternich saw his principles contested was Germany. Not only did he oppose the establishment of constitutional governments here, but he felt that the people themselves were not suited to a unified rule. He believed that German sentiments were too strongly attached to the small political units, that particularism was still the dominant trait in the German's attitude toward his political world. Indeed at the time Metternich was probably correct. The first revolutionary movements were directed against repressive regimes and in favor of constitutional government, with less emphasis on the issue of national unification. The Germanic Confederation as the basis of the organization of the German area was also favored by the middle states such as Bavaria, Hanover, Baden, Württemberg and the two Hesses. Its loose organization protected the independence of the smaller powers and maintained a political balance among them. Austrian predominant influence was usually accepted since it was obvious that the empire wished to preserve conditions as they were and did not wish to extend its power at the expense of the smaller states.

The greatest difficulty the Habsburg Empire met in the Germanies was the Prussian competition for influence and control. A great power in her own right, Prussia had national interests and goals independent of those of Vienna. In 1815 Prussia had made two gains that were not significant at the time but were to give Prussia certain advantages as national feeling rose in the Germanies. As has been seen, in 1806 the Holy Roman Empire came to an end. Although by then this institution had lost all practical significance, the Habsburg rulers, who held the title Holy Roman Emperor, had enjoyed a symbolic primacy among the German princes and had represented at least the shadow of a German nation. A later Prussian ruler, Frederick William IV, was to be greatly attracted by the idea. By losing this position the Habsburg Empire was deprived of one of the bases of its predominance among the German states. In addition, despite the fact that the abandonment of the former Habsburg Rhenish lands at the Congress of Vienna was an advantage for Austrian internal administration, this action left Prussia, with her Rhineland possessions, not the Habsburg Empire, the main defender of the German area against the traditional French opponent. A second basis of the Austrian claim to leadership was thus abandoned.

Prussia was also far better suited to accept and make use of the new political principles. After her complete defeat in the battle of Jena in 1806, Prussia had gone through a period of great national revival and regeneration. Frederick William III was not unfavorable toward some forms of liberal government, and in 1815 he promised his people a constitution. After 1812 he formed a close association with Alexander I. At the Congress of Vienna he had proved an almost subservient supporter of the tsar's policies. Obviously the combination of Prussia and Russia could seriously impede Habsburg policy in central Europe. Metternich had no desire to come into open conflict with Berlin; Prussia had a role to play in his organization of Europe. Instead he now sought to separate Frederick William III from his close association with St. Petersburg and to convince him of the dangers of political reform.

Even with the restoration of the old order in the Germanies the enthusiasm of the national revival in the last days of the Napoleonic wars lingered on. Moreover, certain governments, notably those of Bavaria, Baden and Saxe-Weimar, retained their liberal institutions. The most obvious sign of continued agitation lay in the actions of the students, particularly in the Protestant universities such as Jena. Here they formed political organizations *(Burschenschaften)* and gymnastic societies *(Turnverein)* that carried on revolutionary activities. They adopted the slogan "Liberty, Honor and Fatherland" and the colors red, black and gold, which were now associated with the German national movement. The greatest manifestation they were able to organize was the Wartburg Festival, held in October 1817. Here a group of about 700 students and liberals gathered to celebrate the Reformation and the Battle of Leipzig. During the meeting the crowd became increasingly excited and the gathering came to a climax with the burning of books and certain emblems associated with militarism and reactionary government.

These actions were certainly not proof of a widespread revolutionary conspiracy, nor were they a danger to the established governments. Nevertheless Metternich was able to use them to influence

Frederick William III and to frighten him into hesitating to introduce further reforms in Prussia. In 1819 more serious evidence of revolutionary activity appeared. At this time the anti-nationalist journalist and playwright Ernst Kotzebue was assassinated by Karl Sand, a student at Jena and a member of a secret organization. An attempt was also made on the life of the head of the government of Nassau. Because of these and other incidents, Metternich was able to persuade Frederick William III to join with him in instituting general repressive measures aimed at the revolutionary movement in Germany.

In the summer of 1819 Metternich and the Prussian king met at Teplitz. Here they agreed on a plan to combat revolutionary activity. Their program was then presented at a meeting of representatives from the major German states, which was held in Karlsbad in September. Strong controls were to be introduced in the German schools and universities, over professors as well as students. Publications were to be censored and a central commission was to be set up at Mainz to investigate revolutionary activity. These regulations were accepted by the diet of the Germanic Confederation in the same month. They were to remain in force for five years; at the end of this time they were renewed.

In November 1819 another conference was held in Vienna. The Vienna Final Act of May 1820 strengthened the provisions of the Karlsbad decrees, although it did not go as far as Metternich would have liked. Nevertheless, by this time the Austrian minister had gained the means to combat and control the agencies of change in the Germanies. Whether or not his strong actions were justified by the relative insignificance of the revolutionaries' activities is not important. Metternich was not as concerned with the actions of these groups as he was with the tendency of certain of the German princes to look with sympathy upon liberal reform and to make changes in their governments themselves. He thus used the few signs of revolt to try to persuade these rulers, Frederick William III in particular, to withhold further action in this direction.

Castlereagh sent his personal approval of the measures undertaken. He, like the British government, supported the Austrian predominance in central Europe as a balance against Russia. Similar regulations, the Six Acts, had been introduced in Britain in this same period. In contrast Alexander I expressed his strong dissent. He valued his influence in the German middle states and his close connections with certain courts, such as Bavaria and Württemburg, who were more sympathetic toward liberal reform. He feared that Austria was using the threat of revolution as an excuse to strengthen her hold on the German states. Therefore in January 1820 the Russian government issued a circular opposing the principles of the new system. Metternich always tended to blame Alexander's apparently liberal inclinations on the influence of his Greek minister, John Capodistrias, whom the Austrian statesman disliked with particular intensity.

The Challenge in Italy and Spain

Although Metternich was thus able to bring the German rulers together to cooperate on repressive measures against revolutionary activity in Germany, he was soon to encounter in Italy a challenge to his system that could not so easily be met and that had far wider international repercussions. The maintenance of its Italian possessions was very important to the house of Habsburg. Throughout their history the German princes had been constantly drawn to the south, much as the Russian tsars had been attracted toward Constantinople. After the Congress of Vienna, as we have seen, the Habsburg government attained a predominating position in the peninsula. The two wealthiest Italian provinces, Lombardy and Venetia, were Austrian possessions. They were combined into a joint kingdom. The Habsburg officials made a great effort to set up a really good administration here and to attract the support of the Italian people. Although Austrian rule was indeed an improvement on any previous regime established in the area, it did not succeed in its chief aim. The province was administered from Vienna; too many non-Italian officials were sent in from other parts of the empire.

Although Metternich was not able to form the Italian league he desired, he was able to negotiate special treaties with Tuscany, Modena and, most important, the Kingdom of the Two Sicilies. King Ferdinand I promised that he would introduce no changes in his government without the consent of Austria and that he would not grant a constitution. The Habsburg Monarchy also had close relations with the government of the Papal States. Through these treaties and the strong Austrian military and strategic position in Lombardy-Venetia, control of the peninsula seemed assured. However here, as in the German states, the underground revolutionary

ferment continued. Again the aim of the leaders of the movement
was the overthrow of the extremely bad governments of some of the
Italian states, in particular those of the Kingdom of the Two Sicilies
and the Papal States.

The ordered world of monarchical Europe was first disturbed in
January 1820 by a revolt in Spain. Ferdinand VII was forced at
this time to restore the Spanish constitution of 1812. Here then was
a clear case of a legitimate monarch forced by revolutionary activity
to introduce constitutional government. Alexander I, greatly excited,
wished immediate action. He had been willing to allow the German
rulers to introduce reform on their own initiative, but this violent
action, he believed, called for intervention. The reaction of the
Austrian minister was quite the opposite. Although in Germany Metternich had strongly supported intervention, he remained opposed
to a similar action in Spain. This attitude was also adopted by
Castlereagh. Metternich and the British foreign secretary looked
on the problem in the same manner. Neither wished French or
Russian armies to enter Spain, since intervention would be followed by occupation, and occupation could mean political control.
Castlereagh in the State Paper of 1820, one of the most famous
British statements of policy, expressed his country's refusal to inter-
fere in the domestic affairs of other nations by force. Britain and
Austria thus stood together on the Spanish issue.

In July 1820 the revolutionary forces won another victory—this
time within the Habsburg sphere. A revolt in Naples forced Ferdinand I to grant a constitution. A new regime was established with
relatively little difficulty. Before his people Ferdinand I appeared to
have accepted his role as a constitutional monarch, but behind the
back of the new government he issued appeals for aid to the other
monarchs. For Metternich quite different issues were involved in the
Kingdom of the Two Sicilies than in Spain. The Austrian government felt it could not maintain its hold on the peninsula if a liberal
and revolutionary regime held control in the south. Although Metternich had a low opinion of Ferdinand I as a ruler, he nevertheless
regarded the Neopolitan king as the legitimate sovereign of the
state. In his actions against the revolution Metternich received the
support of the other Italian rulers. The revolutionary challenge was
primarily liberal, not national. All of the Italian princes, including
Victor Emmanuel I of Piedmont, feared for their own power.

To meet this new situation Metternich wished to send Austrian
armies to intervene on the basis of the agreement between the Habs-

burg Empire and the Kingdom of the Two Sicilies. He wanted this
to be an Austrian action, without the participation of the other
powers, although with their approval. He was supported by Castlereagh, who opposed European cooperation for such a task but favored the maintenance of Austrian dominance in Italy. France and
Russia took a different stand. They argued that the powers should
intervene together and that the action should have a European character. They were also not against a compromise with the constitutional regime in Naples. When forced to choose between cooperation
with London or St. Petersburg, Metternich was compelled to follow
the inclinations of his powerful eastern neighbor and accept the
idea of a European congress. He feared that a break with the tsar
would have the effect of drawing France and Russia more closely
together. He thus joined Alexander I in order to control his actions
more effectively.

The Congress of Troppau of October 1820 was primarily an affair
of the three conservative powers; Britain and France sent only ob-
servers. By this time Alexander I had moved to the right. He con-
fided to Metternich that he now regretted his past actions:

> You do not understand why I am no longer the same, I am going
> to tell you. Seven years have passed between 1813 and 1820, and
> these seven years appear to me a century. I would at no price do
> in 1820 what I did in 1813. You have not changed, but I have.
> You have nothing to regret; I cannot say that of myself.[7]

The tsar's conservative inclinations were further strengthened
when during the congress he heard of the revolt of the Semenovsky
Regiment in St. Petersburg. He was now convinced that there existed a great revolutionary conspiracy under the direction of a central committee meeting in Paris, which organized revolts throughout
all of Europe. Metternich was thus able to play upon Alexander's
fears just as previously he had been able to work upon those of the
German rulers. At the congress he was successful in bringing the
tsar to support his policy of opposition to all constitutional systems.
In turn, in the Troppau protocol he accepted Alexander's doctrine
of intervention, although he continued subsequently to support its
application only when it was to Habsburg advantage.

---

[7] Clemens von Metternich-Winneburg, *Mémoires laissé par le Prince de Metternich* (Paris: E. Plon, 1881), III, 374.

In addition, at Troppau the three Eastern powers agreed on intervention in Naples. It was decided that another meeting would be held to which Ferdinand I would be invited. These decisions were all accepted by Frederick William III, who played a largely passive role at the meeting. France remained neutral, though sympathetic; Britain, as we have seen, opposed joint action. When the invitation to Ferdinand I arrived in Naples the wily king was able to persuade his parliament to allow him to attend. Once out of the country he promptly denounced the revolutionary regime.

The Congress of Laibach of January 1821 was another diplomatic victory for Metternich. Here the Austrian minister was able to influence both Alexander I and Ferdinand I. At this meeting the tsar received news of a revolt that had broken out in Moldavia. This event, which commenced the Greek revolution, will be discussed in greater detail in a succeeding section. Metternich was able to convince the tsar that this revolution, whose origins were quite complicated, was nothing more than a revolt of disobedient subjects against their legitimate Ottoman ruler. As expected, Austria at the congress received the mandate to intervene in the Kingdom of the Two Sicilies. At the same time that the Austrian army was engaged in the south, a revolt broke out in Piedmont. This movement was subsequently suppressed by Habsburg forces assisted by Piedmontese troops loyal to the monarch. Because of his great success in this affair Metternich was awarded the title of chancellor, a rank held previously only by the great diplomat Kaunitz.

Although the problem of revolution in Italy was thus solved, that of Spain remained. France now wished to intervene here as Austria had in Naples; Ferdinand VII also requested such action. Metternich maintained his former attitude; he was willing to denounce the revolt in the strongest of terms, but he did not want French armies in Madrid. Again his opinions were shared by Castlereagh. Alexander I continued to argue for intervention. The tsar preferred that a European army carry out the action; he was quite prepared to contribute a large contingent. However, the idea of Russian forces marching across Europe had little appeal to the other European powers. Russia too was willing to accept the proposal that France alone should receive the European mandate. As a result, by April 1823, with the assistance of the French armies, Ferdinand VII regained his former authority. With this action legitimate governments once again held power throughout Europe.

In August 1822 Castlereagh committed suicide, an act that was to have great influence on Austrian relations with Britain. As has been shown, Metternich and Castlereagh had been able to cooperate closely; they had a similar interest in the maintenance of the balance of power. During Castlereagh's ministry the British government had opposed the doctrine of intervention, but it had taken a stand against revolution and had approved of the Austrian position of predominance in Germany and Italy. George Canning, Britain's new foreign minister, was to prove of another disposition. The British attitude now shifted toward a greater willingness to support revolutionary regimes, especially when their victory was in the British interest. Firm opposition was thus offered to any attempt to restore the Spanish colonies in South America to Ferdinand VII. In the future more sympathy was to be shown toward the revolutionary movements in Italy, Greece, Spain, Portugal and Germany, even though active assistance was not offered. This situation became even more marked during the long period when Palmerston and the British Liberal party were in power. Now France and Britain tended to act more often together in international affairs against the alignment of the three conservative powers of the Holy Alliance. These combinations among the powers fluctuated with specific events, but certainly after the death of Castlereagh Austria and Britain did not cooperate as effectively in continental affairs, although they usually supported similar aims in the Near East.

The congresses of Troppau, Laibach and Verona marked a peak in Metternich's career. Although he was unable to gain all he wished, he did obtain the cooperation of the majority of the powers in preserving the status quo in both international relations and in the internal affairs of the European states. He not only saw the revolutionary movements suppressed, but he was able to discourage the acceptance or establishment of constitutional forms of government by the rulers. As long as Alexander I lived, Metternich was able to exert much personal influence over the direction of Russian policy. Frederick William III also never adopted an active and independent stand in international affairs. However, with the passage of time Metternich's position weakened. We have seen how with the death of Castlereagh he lost an important point of support.

In 1825 Alexander I died and was succeeded by his brother Nicholas I, a man of much more decided opinions and character. Of highly conservative inclinations, the new tsar was to take the leadership in the suppression of European revolutions. He, not Metternich, became the driving force within the alignment of the conservative courts. The change in Metternich's position was clearly shown in the events surrounding the Greek revolution of the 1820s, which will be described in another chapter. In this crisis the Austrian minister lost completely his ability to control the course of European international relations; Austria found herself pushed aside from the main currents of diplomatic activity. However, with the settlement of this problem and the revival of revolutionary activity throughout Europe, Metternich was again in a position to influence European affairs.

The Revolutions of 1830

The calm reestablished in central and western Europe by 1823 was abruptly shattered in 1830 by a wave of revolutionary activity that far surpassed that of 1820 in intensity and in its diplomatic repercussions. This time the movement commenced in Paris, where the Bourbon king Charles X was replaced by Louis Philippe of the house of Orleans. This action was obviously the most important victory of the revolutionary forces after the Congress of Vienna. Louis Philippe based his rule on the sovereignty of the people, and he had come to power through forceful and violent means. By chance, at the time of the revolt Metternich and the Russian foreign minister Nesselrode were both in Bohemia. They met at Karlsbad and agreed that they would not intervene in French affairs unless there was a danger of a revival of aggressive French action abroad. Nicholas I, while he did not countermand his minister's actions, was for far more decisive measures. He was, however, unsuccessful not only in gaining the agreement of the powers to intervene in France but even in blocking the recognition of the new regime.

The events in Paris were followed swiftly by an uprising by the Belgians against their Dutch ruler, William I. He, like other monarchs faced with a revolt, immediately issued a call for help. Again the ruler of Russia was eager to act. Metternich was now more worried about what might happen in Italy and did not wish to send Austrian troops to the Low Countries when they might be needed in an area more important to his country's interests. In fact, both Metternich and Nicholas I were soon to show themselves willing to accept a change in the status of the Belgian territories. They preferred to see the Kingdom of the Netherlands separated into a

Dutch and a Belgian state, with William I remaining as the monarch of both sections. In this manner some of the demands of the revolution would be met, but the legitimate ruler would keep his titles intact. The fate of Belgium was a matter of more direct concern to Britain and France than to the three conservative courts. The problem of the Low Countries had always been an important consideration of British policy; the chief aim was to prevent a French absorption of this strategic area. The British government was quite willing to accept a free Belgium, but not one under French control. It was on this basis that an agreement was finally reached among the powers. An independent Belgium, under the rule of Leopold of Saxe-Coburg, was established; this settlement was then imposed upon William I. The creation of the Belgian state was a major break in the settlement of 1815 and the first clear victory of the national principle in western and central Europe after the Congress of Vienna. Austria and Russia, although they would have preferred another arrangement, did not regard the fate of the Low Countries as directly affecting their own real interests.

Moreover, even if the three eastern powers had wished to take a stronger stand, they were prevented from doing so by the outbreak of revolutionary activities on their own doorsteps. Most important was the Polish revolution, which commenced in November 1830. All three of the powers of the Holy Alliance were directly affected because of their common possession of Polish territories. The reaction of the tsar to the revolt could be expected; Nicholas I regarded Congress Poland as an integral part of the Russian state no matter what the constitutional form of the connection was. Although the revolt did not affect the lands under Austrian or Prussian rule, the danger always existed that the movement would spread. Prussia had a vital interest in the suppression of Polish nationalism because of the strategic importance of her Polish territories to the unity of her state. The Austrian government had no intention of surrendering Galicia, and all national movement was regarded as a danger to its own internal order. Nevertheless, for all the German rulers the Polish revolt involved other considerations. The Polish struggle against Russian control aroused much interest and enthusiasm in central Europe. The German liberals naturally welcomed and supported an action in line with their own beliefs. In the Habsburg Monarchy much sympathy was expressed even among strongly conservative circles. The Polish aristocracy from Galicia had come to play a major part in Austrian affairs; they were obviously conservative in their political views and were also strong Catholics. Moreover, although Austria and Russia were cooperating in European affairs, the monarchy, as the weaker partner, was not unhappy to see its neighbor hurt. Throughout the revolt the Austrian government stationed troops on its Polish frontier, kept the border closed and adopted a policy of strict neutrality. After a bitter and difficult campaign the Russian government was finally able to suppress the rebellion. Thereafter another system of government was introduced into Poland through the Organic Statute of 1832. The new regime, in which the Poles lost many of the rights of self-government that they had previously enjoyed, brought increased discontent in the country. Galicia, where the Polish nobility virtually ran their own affairs, continued to be a center of Polish national life.

Although the major revolutionary movements took place in France, Belgium and Poland, there were also uprisings in Italy and manifestations of liberal sympathy in the Germanies. Despite the failure of the revolts of 1820 in the Italian peninsula, agitation and organization for revolt continued. The activities of the secret societies, especially the Carbonari, were now of particular importance. They actively promoted the organization of insurrections against the repressive governments of the peninsula and against Austrian interference. In 1831, inspired by the events in France, uprisings occurred in Parma, Modena and the Papal States. Once again Metternich prepared to move Austrian armies into Italy. By now, however, the international scene had changed. France was in a stronger position and could attempt to reassert her former influence in the Italian states. The movement of Austrian troops into Parma, Modena and the Papal States led to a counteraction by the French and their occupation of Ancona. No general war ensued because the issues were simply not worth a conflict. Louis Philippe had not been in office long enough to risk fighting; he thus refused to support the Italian revolutionary cause. The Austrian government also had a potent weapon that it could use against the French monarch in the person of Napoleon's son, the Duke of Reichstadt, who lived in Vienna. It was recognized that an Orleanist ruler could not long hold out if opposed by a Bonaparte.

The Austrian army thus restored order in the peninsula; again the Italian rulers supported the action. The kings of both Sicily and Piedmont continued to fear the revolutionary forces. In addition,

Piedmont had no desire to see a reassertion of French influence in the peninsula. Victor Emmanuel I therefore made a secret agreement with Austria directed against France. Austrian predominance was now clearly reestablished. Events in Germany followed a similar course. Strong revolutionary activity occurred in Brunswick, Hanover, Hesse-Cassel and Saxony. Student enthusiasm led to the holding of meetings and demonstrations where revolutionary songs and slogans abounded. The most important manifestation was the Hambach National Festival of May 1832. Here between 25,000 and 35,000 enthusiastic students and liberals gathered to listen to speeches urging them to action and, if necessary, to open revolt. These activities gave Metternich the excuse to move. As he did in the earlier period, he met this revolutionary agitation by pressing restrictive measures through the diet of the Germanic Confederation. The Six Articles now passed by this body, like the preceding Karlsbad decrees, were directed toward the suppression of the revolutionary movement. The controls were further strengthened after a group of revolutionaries, chiefly students from the universities of Heidelberg, Würzburg and Erlangen, attempted to seize the city of Frankfurt in a mad escapade. With the failure of this action the German states, like the Italian, returned to normal. In the next years Metternich continued to exert his influence to combat any attempt by a German ruler to introduce liberal measures on his own authority.

The revolutions of 1830 had the great effect of bringing the three Eastern powers closer together. It was now apparent that Austria and Russia had need of each other's assistance. Austria required Russian support in maintaining the status quo in the German and Italian lands; the tsar needed aid in regard to Poland. At München-grätz in September 1833 Russia and the Habsburg Empire signed an agreement that marked the reaffirmation of the Holy Alliance, an alignment that had been weakened by the events in the Near East. In this treaty the two governments guaranteed each other's possessions and reemphasized their support of the principle of intervention. The agreement also covered the Near East and Poland. In October the Prussian government adhered to a part of this pact. The alignment of the three courts was to remain firm until the Crimean War. The powers were now to cooperate not only in Europe, but also in the Near East, an area that was a center of crisis and turmoil in the 1820s and 1830s.

Chapter 3

The Eastern Question

Although after the suppression of the revolutions of the 1820s central Europe was again stable and calm, quite an opposite condition existed in the Balkans. Here events of a liberal, revolutionary character occurred that threatened to upset the European equilibrium. Throughout the nineteenth century one of the chief issues in European diplomacy was the Eastern Question. This phrase referred to the problems in international relations brought about by the decay of the Ottoman Empire and the desire of its subject Christian nationalities to attain political independence. The strategic location of these territories made their fate of first importance to the great powers, in particular to Britain, Russia and Austria. All were concerned lest one of their number should obtain control of the entire area or domination of the Ottoman government.

One of the chief contributions of the Habsburg monarchy to European history had been its role in the prevention of the penetration of Ottoman power deeper into central Europe. Twice Turkish armies had reached the gates of Vienna, but the Habsburg forces had been able to withstand the attack. After the second seige in 1683 the Ottoman Empire was never again able to mount a major offensive against Europe. Instead it was now forced on the defensive by combined Austrian and Russian action. The first major

Austrian gains were made in the Treaty of Karlowitz of 1699. Here the empire won possession of a vast amount of territory—Transylvania, Hungary, Croatia and Slavonia. In subsequent treaties Austria obtained the province of Bukovina and further lands to the southeast. After the treaty of Sistova in 1791 the Habsburg desire for expansion ended. Russia, who had made parallel gains, usually in close cooperation with Austria, continued to exert pressure on the Ottoman Empire. In the Treaty of Bucharest of 1812 the Russian boundary was extended to the Danube River through the acquisition of Bessarabia. Previously, in the Treaty of Kuchuk Kainarji in 1774, Russia secured Ottoman recognition of her special position in the Danubian Principalities and what was later interpreted as a general right to speak in behalf of Balkan Orthodox Christianity.

As we have seen, questions regarding the Ottoman Empire were not discussed at the Congress of Vienna. The Treaty of Bucharest had settled the boundaries between Russia and Turkey. Metternich hoped that peace and stability would return to this area as well as to the rest of Europe. The maintenance of the Ottoman Empire, without a further loss of territory or of power, appeared to him necessary for the protection of the balance of power in eastern Europe. Austria had obviously nothing to gain from a further partition of Ottoman lands. The territories adjacent to the empire were poor and backward, and their acquisition would only increase the empire's internal problems. Any extension of Austrian territory would of necessity be paralleled by a similar increase in Russian influence, which would be extremely detrimental to Habsburg interests. Fortunately for Metternich, Alexander I had much the same attitude toward the Eastern Question. After 1815 he too wished to maintain the status quo in the area.

Despite the fact that the two great powers most concerned were in agreement on the upholding of the Ottoman Empire, the actions of the Balkan subject peoples were to make this policy impossible to follow. As Turkey's power declined, her administration became increasingly corrupt and inefficient. Four hundred years of subjection to Moslem control had not smothered the flames of Christian resistance. Moveover, the ideology of the French Revolution had entered the Balkans through the activities of the merchant class, which was in touch with the major European intellectual currents. Napoleon's formation of the Illyrian Provinces had also a great effect on Balkan national awakening. Before this the wars in the eighteenth century between Russia and Austria against the Ottoman Empire had kept alive the hope that the great powers would continue to fight until the Turkish armies were driven completely out of Europe.

The Habsburg Empire could hope to make no positive gains from the revolt of the Christian peoples. They were in the majority Slavic; their religion was Orthodox, not Catholic. In contrast, Russia could expect to benefit from a revolutionary situation in the Balkans. In the past the people had naturally turned to Russia for aid and protection. From the time of Peter the Great the Russian government had encouraged this reaction; it had often previously called upon the Christian populations for aid in the wars against the Turks. In the Treaty of Kuchuk Kainarji the Russian claim to be the protector of eastern Christianity had been expressed in a veiled form. Should the Balkan states become free, Russia could hope to exert great influence in the area. Moreover, since Russia's assistance was offered in the name of common Orthodoxy there was little contradiction between her aid to Balkan Christianity and her abhorrence of European liberal revolutions. Revolts aimed at freeing Christians from Moslem oppression could be viewed in quite a different light from those whose purpose was the dethronement of a legitimate monarch. In fact, the support of Balkan revolt in the future was to become the main concern of highly conservative and reactionary, as well as liberal, circles in Russian society.

In its desire to maintain the Ottoman Empire and to prevent further Russian encroachment, the Austrian government should have enjoyed the full support of Britain. Austria opposed the growth of Russian power in the Balkans because of its strategic implications for her own lands; Britain feared for her communications with her empire. Nevertheless, the two powers were not able to cooperate effectively in most of the major crises because of certain basic contradictions in their general policies. After the death of Castlereagh, as has been seen, Britain and Austria differed on European policies. Even more important were the military considerations. In its relations with the Ottoman Empire the British government made full use of the influence it could wield through its dominant naval power in the eastern Mediterranean. It had no land forces of importance that it could employ in the area. In the repeated crises in the Near East in the nineteenth century Britain would have been glad to have been able to make use of Habsburg military power to check a possible Russian advance on Constantinople. The Austrians, naturally, were not so eager to become the instrument of the attainment of British aims, particularly since they generally believed that alone they could not defeat the Russian armies. Austria's position was thus most difficult. Her aims in the Balkans usually coincided with those of Britain, and also France. She did not wish to see a further extension of Russian power, but she could not afford to be placed in a position where her armies would be forced to fight Russia to protect British and French imperial and Mediterranean interests.

In every major Balkan crisis Austria thus faced unpleasant alternatives. She did not want a Russian advance in the Balkans; she feared the national movements in the Ottoman Empire because of their possible effects on her own nationality problem. However here, as in central Europe, she could not stop the progress of events. With time the revolutionary activity increased in strength and vigor. Under these circumstances the chief problem that faced the Habsburg Empire was how to prevent Russia from exploiting this situation to gain an overwhelming predominance in the area. Many methods were used during the century. Metternich first tried to persuade the tsar that any Balkan revolt should be classified as a revolution against a legitimate sovereign. This approach was to prove more effective with Alexander I than with Nicholas I. At the time of the Crimean War Austria tended to favor France and Britain against Russia and as a result gained the disdain and distrust of all three. Later in the century an attempt was made to achieve a division of the Balkans into Austrian and Russian spheres of influence. This method failed because of the difficulties inherent in any such arrangement. Austria's military weakness and her fear of risking a war with her great neighbor hampered her actions at all times.

The first Balkan revolt that achieved success, that in Serbia, broke out during the Napoleonic wars. The insurgent leaders first appealed to Vienna for aid. When it was denied them, they turned to St. Petersburg. Although the Russian government at first promised assistance, the events in Europe and the invasion of 1812 prevented it from carrying out this policy. In 1813 Ottoman forces put down the revolt. A second uprising in 1815 was more successful. Serbia now gained an autonomous regime largely because of Russian pressure on the Turkish government. These events had few repercussions in Europe. Serbia was a virtually unknown, backward province of the Ottoman Empire. Her fate in no way involved the balance of power in Europe.

The Greek revolution of the 1820s was quite a different matter, and it was to cause the major diplomatic controversy of the decade. In March 1821 Alexander I at the Congress of Laibach received news that a revolt against Ottoman rule had begun in Moldavia, led by Greek forces under the leadership of Prince Alexander Ypsilanti, an officer in the Russian army. The rebels at once appealed for Russian aid. Although Metternich was at first not much impressed by the event, he soon recognized the dangers in the situation. Capodistrias, whom the Austrian minister greatly disliked, was deeply involved in Greek affairs and had in fact been previously offered the leadership of the Greek movement. Metternich thus used all his influence with the tsar to try to persuade him that this revolt was exactly like those that the conservative powers were attempting to suppress in the rest of Europe. Alexander I, strongly impressed by Metternich's arguments, denounced the revolution and struck Ypsilanti's name from the Russian army list. He also approved Turkish armed intervention in the Principalities. Deprived of Russian support, the Greek revolt in the Rumanian lands soon collapsed. Ypsilanti died in an Austrian prison.

The Ottoman suppression of the rebellion in the Principalities did not bring an end to the Greek question. Simultaneously an uprising had taken place in the Morea, which was to prove beyond the power of the Turkish government to handle. In Greece proper the rebels were aided by the sympathetic support of their countrymen and by the difficult terrain, which made it impossible for the Turkish armies to operate effectively. As the revolt continued it gained increasingly more attention in Europe. Throughout the continent educated Europeans, particularly those with liberal or romantic inclinations, were deeply stirred by the rebellion of the modern Greeks, whom they equated with the Greeks of their own classical studies, against a Moslem, Asiatic overlord. Philhellenism was to become a real political force throughout Europe. In Britain it was to prove an important factor leading to eventual British support of Greek independence. In Austria, too, ardent sympathy was felt for the cause of Greek freedom.

The international tension attendant on the revolt was increased by the Ottoman reaction to the events and the violent reprisals that were taken against Greek populations, whether they were guilty or not of revolutionary actions. The height of Ottoman terror was the hanging of the patriarch of Constantinople and some of his bishops on Easter night. This measure caused a great reaction in Russia, the patron of Balkan Orthodoxy, and a real crisis occurred. The Russian government was also in conflict with the Porte[8] over questions dealing with the Caucasian frontier and the Turkish actions in the Principalities.

The danger of the situation was recognized by Metternich and Castlereagh, both of whom feared the consequences of a war between Russia and the Ottoman Empire. Metternich continued to hope that the Greek revolt would die out or that the Ottoman troops would crush it. In October 1821 Metternich met Castlereagh and George IV in Hanover to discuss the Greek affair. Neither foreign minister wished a Greek victory or a Russian unilateral intervention. The British and Austrian governments both urged moderation toward the Porte.

The immediate crisis was bridged because the Ottoman government did indeed take measures to calm the situation. Moreover, Alexander I did not want a war; the immediate issues between Russia and the Porte were not that serious. The tsar continued to feel no sympathy with the Greek rebels. Capodistrias left the Russian service in 1822 and went to Switzerland where he continued to work for the Greek cause. Alexander I commented at this time on the situation:

> If we reply to the Turks with war, ... the Paris directing committee will triumph and no government will be left standing. I do not intend to leave a free field to the enemies of order. At all costs means must be found of avoiding war with Turkey.[9]

At this time the tsar also proposed the setting up of three Greek principalities, similar to the Rumanian provinces, which would have autonomous rights. To both Austria and Britain this proposal appeared the equivalent of the establishment of a Russian satellite Greece. Metternich suggested instead the formation of an independent Greece in the belief that such a state would be more capable of resisting Russian pressure.

---

[8] The Ottoman government was often referred to in diplomatic correspondence as *the Porte*. The term Sublime Porte refers to the gateway leading to the building that housed the principal offices of the government in Constantinople.

[9] Matthew S. Anderson, *The Eastern Question, 1774–1923* (New York: St. Martins, 1966), p. 61.

Despite the lessening of the danger of war between Russia and the Ottoman Empire, the problem of the Greek rebellion remained. For Metternich the entire matter had become a nightmare. In 1822 a Greek revolutionary government declared the independence of the country and proceeded to formulate a very liberal constitution. Castlereagh had now been succeeded by Canning. Although this statesman too supported the maintenance of the Ottoman Empire, he was more swayed by British public opinion than was his predecessor. Britain recognized the Greek rebels as belligerents, and in 1824 private loans became available to the insurgent government.

Unable to crush the revolt with its own forces, the Ottoman government was forced to call for aid from its vassal, Mohammed Ali, the pasha of Egypt. Egyptian forces first crushed the rebellion in Crete and then in 1825 crossed to the Greek mainland. In the same year Nicholas I replaced Alexander I and inaugurated a more vigorous policy. He now separated the Russian disagreements with the Porte on Rumanian and Caucasian matters from the Greek affair. The first set of questions continued to be a matter for bilateral negotiation between Constantinople and St. Petersburg; the Greek revolt, in contrast, the tsar intended to settle in agreement with the Western powers.

Approaches had already been made between Britain and Russia before the death of Alexander I. Canning, who favored cooperation with Russia, used the occasion of the coronation of the tsar to send the Duke of Wellington to Russia to negotiate. In 1826 the Protocol of St. Petersburg was signed; here Russia and Britain agreed to work together in the Greek affair and to try to obtain the establishment of an autonomous Greek state. Having made this agreement with Britain on the Greek issue, Nicholas I continued to press the Porte to fulfill his demands on the matters in conflict between them. Fearing war, both Britain and Austria urged the Porte to make concessions. Unable to gain support abroad and in the midst of a reform of his armed forces, Sultan Mahmud was compelled in October 1826 to sign the Convention of Akkerman, which fulfilled the Russian demands.

After the signature of the Protocol of St. Petersburg, Britain and Russia sought to obtain the adherence of the other powers to the agreement. France accepted, and in 1827 the Treaty of London between the three states was concluded. Prussia and Austria, however, remained outside of this combination. The Holy Alliance thus broke down on Balkan affairs; Metternich found himself isolated and without influence in the settlement of a Balkan problem of concern to Austria.

Once the three allied powers had established their policy of cooperation they proceeded to act together to end the Greek revolt according to their terms. In October 1827 a combined allied force caught a Turkish fleet in the Bay of Navarino. Fighting broke out, and in the resultant confusion the Turkish ships were sunk. Not only was Metternich deeply shocked by this event, but the Duke of Wellington, who had replaced Canning as foreign minister, denounced the entire affair. The enraged Ottoman government now declared a Holy War on Russia. France, Britain and Austria were forced to stand aside and allow the Porte and Russia to go to war, a situation that these powers had previously sought to prevent.

Contrary to Austrian and British fears, the Russo-Turkish War of 1828–1829, although resulting in a Russian victory, did not lead to a severe diminution of the power of the Ottoman Empire. Prior to the signing of the Treaty of Adrianople in 1829, the Russian government came to the conclusion that the continued existence of the Turkish state was to its benefit. It was decided that the attempt would be made to dominate the Ottoman government but not to destroy or partition its territories. In the peace treaty Russia did nevertheless gain important concessions. Serbia and the Danubian Principalities had their autonomous rights confirmed, but they were placed specifically under Russian protection. In addition, Russia took the mouth of the Danube, including the Sulina Channel, the one navigable arm of the river at this point. The agreement also provided that Greece was to be set up as an autonomous state.

The Austrian government was thus forced to witness changes in the Balkan peninsula that were made without its participation or consent. The Russian position in the Danubian Principalities and on the Danube was considerably strengthened. The Habsburg Monarchy took no part in the establishment of the small but independent Greek state that was now set up. The allied powers also chose its ruler, Otto, the second son of the king of Bavaria. In subsequent years the Greek government was to be influenced chiefly by the states responsible for its existence. Greece, in contrast to the Danubian Principalities, was not, however, a vital area for Austria.

In the next years the Habsburg Empire continued to play a relatively minor role in Eastern affairs. The great antagonists in the area were Britain and Russia. The next crisis concerned the attempt of Mohammed Ali and his son Ibrahim to extend their control over Syria. In 1832 the Egyptian armies defeated the Turkish forces and menaced Constantinople. In this desperate situation Sultan Mahmud appealed to Britain. When that power refused aid, the sultan was forced to turn to Russia. In return for its assistance, in July 1833 the Russian government obtained the very advantageous Treaty of Unkiar Skelessi, which gave Russia a determining voice in Ottoman affairs. However, although Nicholas I had thus won a great diplomatic victory in the Near East, he had at the same time been forced to deal with the dangerous Polish revolt. It was now apparent that he needed to act in cooperation with Vienna and Berlin. In the Convention of Münchengrätz, in addition to the conditions already described, Russia and Austria agreed to unite to oppose any further actions by Mohammed Ali and to support the maintenance of the Ottoman Empire. If a dissolution of that state threatened, the two powers were to consult. As long as Nicholas I stood for the upholding of the status quo in the Balkans, Metternich could work with him. This agreement also gave Austria again an important role in Eastern affairs.

Despite his defeat in 1832 the sultan never gave up the hope of gaining revenge. Mohammed Ali in turn wished to change his lands into a hereditary kingdom. In 1839 the sultan precipitated a new crisis by launching an attack against the Egyptian forces. He was promptly defeated, and the danger existed again that the Ottoman Empire might fall. This time Austria joined with Russia, Britain and Prussia in defense of the Porte. Egypt now had the backing of France, who had gained much influence with Mohammed Ali. Be-. cause of the attitude of France the fear existed for a short while that war would break out on the Rhine, but Louis Philippe was in no position to fight a major war against all of the European powers. In 1841 a peace was made in which the Ottoman Empire received back the Syrian lands it had previously lost to Egypt; Mohammed Ali in return was recognized as hereditary ruler of Egypt.

In 1841 Austria joined with the other powers, including France, in signing the Straits Convention. In this agreement the Straits were placed under international control. Russia at the same time allowed the Treaty of Unkiar Skelessi to lapse. Twenty years of crisis in the

Near East had thus ended in a settlement that Metternich could accept. Although a free Greece had been established and Russia had won a stronger position in the Danubian Principalities and Serbia, the Ottoman Empire remained virtually intact. Moveover, in the Convention of Münchengrätz Metternich had gained Russian assurance that no moves would be made without a prior agreement with the Habsburg Empire.

Chapter 4

Pre-March

The last decade of Metternich's period in office passed quite calmly. The Egyptian question and disturbances in Switzerland and on the Iberian peninsula did not seriously endanger the general peace. For Austria the main event in international relations was her acquisition of the minute Republic of Cracow. Since 1815 this last piece of Polish soil enjoying an independent status had become a center of Polish culture and a haven for political refugees. As such it had been a decided annoyance to the partition powers. Already in 1835 it had been decided by the three emperors that the territory should go to Austria, but a "legitimate" excuse was needed for this violation of the European treaties. The occasion was presented in 1846 when a rebellion occurred in Cracow, as well as in Galicia, which led to the occupation of the city by Austrian troops. On Russian urging and with Prussian consent the Habsburg government proceeded to annex the territory. This action called forth British and French protests since it was in contradiction to the Vienna treaties. The conservative powers had here violated their own principles.

During this period of tranquility it was quite apparent that Metternich had lost much of his former influence in European affairs. His position within the Austrian government had similarly been weakened. In 1835 Emperor Francis died. This monarch had been content with the appearance of power; he had let Metternich determine the lines of policy. Francis I was followed by his son, the mentally deficient Ferdinand I. His accession maintained the Habsburg principles of dynastic succession intact, but the new emperor was not capable of ruling. The direction of the state therefore fell into the hands of a state council composed of Metternich, Archduke Louis, Francis' brother and Count Francis Anton Kolowrat, who was from a Bohemian noble family and whose special field was finance. Kolowrat and Metternich clashed constantly and engaged in continual petty intrigues and quarrels. Metternich, it should be noted, had never been in a position to make internal affairs his particular concern. His attention, even under Francis I, had been directed toward foreign affairs.

Important changes had also occurred in Europe; new men and new problems had arisen. Austrian relations with Britain were never close while Palmerston was in office. Cooperation was possible on Eastern affairs, but seldom in Europe. Among the conservative powers the energetic and decisive leadership was given by the strong-willed Nicholas I. It was he rather than Metternich who continued to stand as the prime spokesman for the old order and the principle of intervention to protect legitimate governments from revolutionary activity.

In the Germanies and Italy too the general situation had altered. In the German area Metternich had always recognized the importance of Prussia. One of his great achievements had been his establishment of domination over Frederick William III, who had been persuaded to give up the idea of granting a constitution and who had not challenged Austria's prime position in the Germanic Confederation. Control of Prussia, the second German state and a military power, was no mean accomplishment since, unlike the Habsburg Empire, this state could make use of new ideas such as German nationalism and liberal economic programs to gain the leadership of the German states.

By the 1830s the Prussian government had completed an action, the significance of which became fully apparent only later. Starting in 1819 Prussia made a series of tariff agreements with her neighbors and then gradually with the other German states. Although much opposition was met, Prussia nevertheless was able to join almost all of the German states to her in a customs union, or *Zollverein*. This combination filled a real need of the rising German economy and gave Prussia a position of leadership in this field. Metternich himself was well aware of the significance of the Zollverein. He would have liked to have associated Austria with it, but the refusal of certain agricultural interests in the empire to accept a tariff reduction made this impossible.

In 1840 a new monarch, Frederick William IV, came to the Prussian throne. In contrast to his predecessor, he was to prove a difficult man for Metternich to handle. Erratic, unstable and impractical, the Prussian king had been much influenced by the spirit of the Romantic age. He had an enormous respect for the Habsburg rulers as the first of the German princes, and he looked back with nostalgia on the German past and the Holy Roman Empire. When he first came to the throne, the liberal elements in Germany were filled with hope because of his early moves toward political reform in Prussia. In the future he was to disappoint them badly.

In Italy similar changes had occurred. In 1846 Austrian-born Pope Gregory VII died, to be succeeded by Pius IX, who was known for his liberal inclinations. In the first part of his period in office he introduced much-needed reforms in the administration of the Papal States. Charles Albert, who became king of Piedmont in 1831, was also looked upon as a possible leader in a future national movement, although his attitude was basically conservative and he was at first hesitating and indecisive. Despite the lack of success in the past the Italian liberal and national movement continued to grow in strength. The Young Italy society of Mazzini was particularly effective in organizing underground activity. Not only was this agitation difficult for the Austrian government to counteract, it always had to consider the British and French attitude. Both of these powers would have been most pleased to see the Austrian expulsion from Italy. France wished to supplant Austrian control with her own; Britain hoped to secure a liberal, reformed Italy who could resist the influence of both of her neighbors.

The Habsburg Monarchy was also faced with increasing national pressures within its own boundaries. Metternich, as has been mentioned, believed that Austria was by her very nature suited only to a federal form of government and that each of her sections should preserve its own unique character and institutions. In the years before 1848 the Magyars, the strongest national group after the Germans, went through a period of national reawakening very similar to that which was simultaneously taking place in the Italian peninsula and the Germanies. Unlike the other territories of the empire, the Hungarian lands formed a distinct kingdom with its own diet of two houses and a strong provincial administrative system. In 1825 the Hungarian diet was summoned for the first time in a decade. Once it had assembled, its members proceeded to challenge Austrian control and agitate for more rights. In 1840 special laws were passed that made Magyar, not Latin, the language of government and administration. At this time Hungarian politics tended to divide into two currents—one associated with the moderate Count Stephen Szechenyi, the other with the more radical Louis Kossuth. In 1847 Kossuth won a decided victory in the elections to the diet. His program strongly affirmed the national demands of the Magyars against the Habsburg Monarchy and the right of the Hungarian government to control all of the so-called Lands of the Crown of St. Stephen, in which the Magyars were in fact a minority of the population. Kossuth thus desired to impose the form of a modern, unitary, Magyar national state upon an area in which about half of the people were either Slavic or Rumanian. The disastrous results of this policy were to be apparent in the internal and foreign relations of the empire until its downfall in 1918.

The years before 1848 were also marked by a strong cultural revival among the Slavic peoples, which was to have important political repercussions both during the revolutions of 1848 and throughout the rest of the century. The rise in general interest in history and in the origins of the various European peoples, connected with the Romantic movement and the work of Herder, assisted in the revival of national consciousness among the intellectuals of the Slavic nations. This trend was especially prominent among the Czechs, but it also affected the Croats, Serbs, Slovaks and Slovenes. Each nationality became increasingly concerned with its own past history, music, folklore, language, customs and traditions. It was to prove but a short step from cultural self-consciousness to increased political awareness.

The period of international calm enjoyed by almost all of the states since the early 1830s was shattered in the revolutionary year 1848. This time the revolt commenced in Italy and then spread to Paris. In February Louis Philippe was forced out and replaced by a revolutionary government. On March 13 Vienna rose in rebellion. After forty years in power Metternich was now forced to flee to England, while the empire, whose foreign affairs he had so long directed, was swept by revolt. The Austrian minister had become the symbol of the system of reaction and repression established in central Europe after 1815. The representatives of the Viennese revolutionary government in demanding Metternich's removal expressed this idea: "Your Excellency, we have nothing against your person, but everything against your system."[10]

Although Metternich was thus forced out of office through revolutionary uprising and court intrigue, he was to return to Vienna in 1851, and his policies were in general those adhered to by succeeding Habsburg foreign ministers. During his long years in office his view of the position of the Habsburg Monarchy among the European powers had been highly realistic; he had adopted the course of action that he felt was best suited to the preservation of a multinational, conservative monarchy menaced by the ambitions of two great powers and by the revolutionary concepts of the age, whose victory he felt would destroy his country and his society. He felt himself the defender of the forces of order against those of disorder and chaos. He had been able to preserve the highly advantageous situation created by the Congress of Vienna by allying the empire with the two powers whose monarchs had a similar interest in preserving the conservative political orientation of central and eastern Europe. Through this alignment he was also able to restrain and control Prussian action in the Germanies and Russian moves in the Balkans. Metternich always understood the close link between internal political ideology and foreign policy. He was able to use his neighbors' fear of revolution, which he too shared, to bring their support behind Habsburg predominance in the Germanies and in the Italian peninsula. Even in the Eastern Question, where he could restrain Russian intervention less easily, the final settlements of the series of crises were not detrimental to Austrian basic interests in the area. No Habsburg minister after Metternich held a similar position within the empire for such a long period of time or exerted such a profound influence on the affairs of Europe.

---

[10] R. Charmatz, *Geschichte der auswärtigen Politik Österreichs im 19. Jahrhundert* (Leipzig: B. G. Teubner, 1918), I, 135.

Part II

The Age of National Unifications:
1848–1870

Chapter 1

The Revolutions of 1848

By March 1848 the entire central European area had fallen to the revolutionary forces. In the Italian and German states new governments everywhere held control. Within the Habsburg Empire the three great cities, Vienna, Budapest and Prague, became centers of revolt, with each representing the movement of one of the major national groups in the empire—the Germans, the Magyars and the Slavs. In Vienna an uprising led by students, workers and middle-class men of liberal, socialist and radical tendencies first forced the Habsburg government to dismiss Metternich. Karl Ludwig Ficquelmont, who now became foreign minister, was a man of similar opinions and had actually been designated by Metternich as his successor.

In the next weeks the court was gradually forced to accept other demands of the revolutionary leaders. In April it issued a constitution, based on the Belgian model, but the new regime in Vienna wished to draw up its own document. A constituent assembly was thus promised. Feeling endangered by the continual agitation and unrest, the court decided to move to Innsbruck. Although control had been lost in Vienna, it should be noticed that the court was still in command of the imperial army, with the exception of the Hungarian sections, and it held the loyalty of the military commanders.

This army now prepared to act first against the revolutionary movement in Italy.

Meanwhile, throughout central Europe delegates were being chosen to participate in the several constituent assemblies that were then being formed. The most successful revolutionary movement was certainly that in Hungary. Here, due to the energetic leadership of Kossuth and the fact that the preceding years had been devoted to preparation for the accomplishment of just such an action, a government was set up that was in practice a separate Hungarian state. The March Laws joined the Hungarian lands to the rest of the empire only through the person of the Habsburg ruler. The Austrian government was forced to accept this arrangement because it was as yet in no position to combat the Hungarian revolution. The rapid formulation of these administrative acts and the establishment of a regular government in Hungary were in contrast to the actions of the delegates to the German assembly at Frankfurt, the Austrian constituent assembly and the Slavic congress in Prague.

The revolutionary forces met their first defeat at Prague. Here on June 2 a congress of delegates from the Slavic peoples of the empire met; this congress had been called as an answer to the German Frankfurt Assembly and was dominated by the Czechs. The tone of the meeting was not anti-Habsburg. Most of the delegates supported the program of Austroslavism, which called for the separate and autonomous organization of the nationalities within the Habsburg Empire, not for its dissolution into national states. After the assembly had been in session only a short while, riots broke out in the streets of the city. General A. Windischgrätz, in command of the army in the district, reacted strongly. He moved his forces into Prague, put an end to its revolutionary government and established a military rule in Bohemia. The Slav Congress was dismissed. This action marked the first significant victory of the court over the revolution. The army had restored Habsburg authority to one section of the empire.

In July 1848 a constituent assembly met in Vienna; the popular Archduke John opened its sessions. The great accomplishment of this body, in fact its only achievement of note, was the emancipation of the peasants. With the fulfillment of this principal aim the peasantry as a group lost interest in the revolution. Meanwhile the forces loyal to the court continued to gain in strength. At the end of July the Austrian army in Italy under the command of General Joseph Radetzky defeated the king of Piedmont at the battle of Custozza. Another step toward the reestablishment of the control of the old government had thus been taken. Despite this gain, a second revolt in Vienna in October forced the court to move to Olmütz; at the same time the parliament was transferred to Kremsier. Windischgrätz marched on Vienna. By the end of October he had reoccupied the city and restored imperial authority.

In November the Habsburg government was greatly strengthened by the appointment as chief minister of Prince Felix Schwarzenberg, a brother-in-law of Windischgrätz, and the last of the great line of Austrian diplomats, which had included Kaunitz and Metternich. A tough, realistic and clever statesman, he was able to secure by his astute diplomatic methods the restoration of Austrian power. At the same time another major change was made in the Habsburg government. It was finally recognized that a feeble-minded sovereign was not suitable as the head of a great state in a time of crisis. Ferdinand I therefore abdicated in favor of his eighteen-year-old nephew, Francis. In order to recall the days of the reforming emperor, Joseph II, this name was added to that of the new ruler. Because of his age and inexperience Francis Joseph in the first years of his reign was largely guided in his actions by his mother, Archduchess Sophia, and by Schwarzenberg. It was only after the death of the minister in 1852 that the emperor took over the real direction of the government.

With a new leadership and with the military accomplishments in Italy and Bohemia behind it, the imperial government was in a better position to deal firmly with the revolutionary elements. During this period the Kremsier parliament had been engaged in drawing up a constitution designed to reconstitute the empire in the manner desired by the revolutionary forces, that is, as a federal union with the real power left in the hands of the provincial authorities. In March 1849 Schwarzenberg dissolved this assembly and issued a constitution of a quite different character. In this document the empire was organized as a highly centralized state, with one administrative system for all of the lands, including Hungary. Although this constitution was abolished in 1851, the centralized administration, to be known as the Bach System, was retained.

Having dealt with these political problems, Schwarzenberg now turned to restoring Habsburg influence in Italy, Hungary and the German states, which were still under revolutionary control. The events described above, involving primarily the internal affairs of the empire, had not been subject to outside intervention. In contrast, in dealing with the situation in these three areas the Habsburg government was faced with the interference of the other great powers, all of whom had special interests to defend. For the sake of clarity the Austrian policy in Italy, Hungary and the Germanies will be discussed separately.

Italy By the end of March 1848 constitutional regimes had been introduced, as a result of revolutionary action, in the Kingdom of the Two Sicilies, Tuscany and Piedmont. In that same month Lombardy and Venetia also rose against Austrian rule. Radetzky and his army were forced back into the fortresses of the Quadrilateral, the strategically strongest point in the Italian peninsula. A republic was set up in Venice. The two provinces immediately appealed to Charles Albert for assistance. The Piedmontese monarch now abandoned his hesitant attitude, and on March 22 entered the struggle against Austria. Although forces from other parts of Italy subsequently joined the Piedmontese army, none of the other Italian states took part in the war openly. Charles Albert himself decided against an appeal for outside assistance. Aid could only be gained from France, and the fear existed that such help would result in the replacement of Austrian with French domination or that a demand for compensation would be made.

In the Germanies and in Hungary the principal outside power to influence the final settlement was Russia; in Italy, Britain and France were able to play a major role in directing the course of events. Although both of these powers were in sympathy with Italian demands for political reform and independence from Austrian interference, they were not united in their actions. The British government under the direction of Lord Palmerston had no desire to see France take the place of Austria in the peninsula. The French government in this critical period was weakened by the fact that it too was a revolutionary regime and its leaders were divided in their aims. Although in theory they stood for the destruction of the settlement of 1815, which was regarded as a stain on French national honor, and they favored national movements, they knew that they were not strong enough to involve themselves in a war with Austria, who might be backed by Britain and Russia. They were also to prove quite realistic in their appraisal of the significance for France of a unified Italy or Germany, or even of an increase in the power and prestige of Charles Albert.

At the beginning of the war in Italy the Habsburg government, severely weakened by the events at home, believed that it would have to make large concessions in Italy. Ficquelmont, the foreign minister, was chiefly worried that France would aid Piedmont, who would then be able to drive Austria out of Italy. He thus turned to Britain. Palmerston had opposed the entrance of Charles Albert into the war, and he shared the same fear of the possible consequences of French intervention. The British foreign secretary therefore pressed the Austrian government to make a peaceful settlement and to come to terms with the revolutionary regimes in Lombardy and Venetia. The Austrian government was willing to allow the two provinces autonomous governments under a Habsburg archduke, but Palmerston wished the empire to surrender all of Lombardy and Venetia to Piedmont. In May 1848 Johann Philip von Wessenberg became the Austrian foreign minister, and he adopted a somewhat stronger attitude. Negotiations were taken up with the revolutionary government in Milan. This regime wanted Austria not only to recognize the independence of Lombardy and Venetia but to surrender the southern Tyrol. These demands awakened strong Austrian resistance. Meanwhile the fighting continued. At Custozza on July 24, as has been mentioned, Radetzky won a major victory over the Piedmontese armies. In the beginning of August the Austrians entered Milan and soon thereafter an armistice was signed with Charles Albert, who withdrew his forces from Lombardy.

Although they had widely different aims in Italy, France and Britain now agreed to cooperate to mediate the Piedmontese-Austrian conflict. They wished to secure Lombardy for Piedmont despite the Habsburg military victory. The Austrian government, in a much stronger position after the military successes against the Prague revolutionary forces and the Piedmontese, preferred to negotiate directly with Turin. It was also determined not to surrender Lombardy. The British stand weakened as its fears gradually increased that France might use the opportunity of a renewal of the war in northern Italy to go to the support of Piedmont. In November, when

Schwarzenberg became minister, the Austrian attitude hardened further. He immediately repudiated British mediation and in a circular expressed his opinion of the British actions:

> Palmerston regards himself too much as the arbiter of Europe. For our part we are not disposed to accord him the role of Providence. We never impose our advice on him in relation to Ireland: let him spare himself the trouble of advising us on the subject of Lombardy.[11]

The tone of Austrian diplomacy now fully reflected the new strength of the imperial government and the improved position of the dynasty as against the revolutionary forces.

In March 1849 Charles Albert gave way before pressure from within his own state and recommenced hostilities. He was encouraged in this action by the success of the Hungarian armies against the Habsburg forces at this time. However, almost immediately at Novara the Austrian forces again defeated the Piedmontese, and Charles Albert was forced to seek another armistice. In the negotiations that followed, the British and the Austrians both remained apprehensive that the French might intervene. The final peace was based on a return to the territorial status quo as it existed before the war, and Piedmont paid an indemnity. After this humiliation Charles Albert was forced to abdicate. His successor, Victor Emmanuel II, kept the constitution that had been introduced into Piedmont at the time of the revolution. Despite its defeat Piedmont in fact gained in prestige among the Italian liberal and national circles. Not only did it retain its constitutional government, it was the only Italian state that had showed itself willing to fight for the national cause.

With the signature of the peace, conditions in Italy gradually returned to normal. The revolt in the Kingdom of the Two Sicilies failed in the spring of 1849. Austrian armies crushed the revolutionary movements in Tuscany and Venetia. The problem of Rome, however, remained. At the end of November 1848 Pius IX was forced to flee the city, and in February 1849 a republic under Mazzini was

---

[11] R. W. Seton-Watson, *Britain in Europe, 1789–1914* (Cambridge: Cambridge University Press, 1955), p. 262.

set up. In December. 1848 Louis Napoleon, a nephew of the great Napoleon, was elected president of France. To assert the French presence on the peninsula he decided to send a force to Rome to restore the pope. In June and July, 1849, a French army corps attacked and then occupied Rome. In 1850 the pope returned, but the French troops were compelled to remain to protect him. This entire expedition was to prove a great embarrassment to France in both internal affairs and international relations.

Hungary   As has been shown, the Austrian government was able to reassert its position in Vienna, Prague and the Italian peninsula through the victories of the imperial army and because of the division of its opponents. Matters were to prove quite different in Hungary, where the efficient and enthusiastic Magyar forces were able to defeat the Habsburg armies and where at least the dominant national group in the area remained united. Even after the acceptance by the Habsburg government of the March Laws, relations between Vienna and Budapest continued to deteriorate. In September 1848 an Austrian army, under the Habsburg-appointed governor of Croatia, Joseph Jelačić, was sent against the Hungarian forces. In the next months the fortunes of war shifted constantly, but the Habsburg armies were not able to crush the Hungarians. In April 1849 the Hungarian Diet declared the state a republic with Kossuth as president. All ties with the Habsburg Empire were now severed.

The Hungarian government after its declaration of independence immediately attempted to gain support from abroad, but with no success. Only the Republic of Venice would recognize the new regime. Britain and France remained aloof. Palmerston, although he desired the end of Austrian influence in Italy, did not want to weaken the monarchy as a great power. He believed that the existence of the empire as a viable and strong political unit was necessary to check the expansion of Russia in central Europe and in the Balkans. It was recognized that should Hungary secede from the empire, Austria would not be able to fulfill that function.

Unable to check the Hungarian revolution alone, the Habsburg government asked for Russian assistance. It has since been much debated whether or not this move was wise or necessary, because of its great repercussions in the future. However it must be remembered that conditions in Italy, Germany and the other parts of the empire were still not stable and that the Habsburg armies were being defeated in Hungary. In the beginning of May 1849 Francis Joseph wrote a personal letter to the tsar asking for assistance based on the principle of intervention to support a monarch threatened by revolutionary activity. Nicholas I agreed at once to the request. He already had an army in Moldavia, which had entered the Danubian Principalities to suppress revolts that had broken out in that area in 1848. He had previously followed the successes of the Hungarian forces with apprehension. Not only did he fear the revolution as such, but he particularly disliked the presence of some 10,000 Polish volunteers in the Hungarian army and the actions of the Polish generals Bem and Dembinski. If he did not intervene he might be faced with a Hungarian state based on revolutionary principles, which would menace his hold on his Polish territories. Moreover, like Britain and France, Russia considered the continued existence of the Austrian state necessary for the European balance of power. His policy was now to seek the reestablishment of the conditions of the prerevolutionary period in central Europe. He thus was to oppose both an independent Hungary and a united Germany.

The entrance of over 150,000 Russian troops into Hungary proved too much for the Hungarian forces. At Vilagos in August 1849 General Görgei surrendered to the Russian General Paskievich and not to the Habsburg commander. The entire campaign and the aftermath caused much friction between the Austrian and Russian armies. The Russians complained at the prices charged for supplies, and they were shocked at the Austrian treatment of the prisoners, particularly at the execution of thirteen Hungarian generals whom the Russian army had handed over to the Habsburg authorities. The Austrian government acted with much greater strictness in Hungary than in Lombardy-Venetia in dealing with former rebels; they even executed Count Kasimir Batthyany, the first Hungarian premier after the March revolution. The Austrian actions were strongly denounced by European opinion, particularly in Britain.

The suppression of the Hungarian revolution also caused a minor Eastern crisis. After the defeat, Kossuth, General Bem and thousands of others fled into the Ottoman Empire. The Russian and Austrian governments demanded their surrender. Backed by Britain and France, the Ottoman government refused. At this time a British squadron entered the Straits in violation of the convention of 1841. Palmerston later apologized for this action. The entire incident was settled when neither Austria nor Russia pressed her demand for the extradition of the fugitives.

Germany With the suppression of the revolt in Hungary the Habsburg government was free finally in the fall of 1849 to exert its influence in the Germanies. By this time the Frankfurt Assembly had collapsed from internal dissension and from the failure of the Prussian government to accept a revolutionary solution to the German problem. As in the rest of central Europe in March 1848, revolutionary regimes had taken control throughout the German states with programs calling for liberal internal reform and the formation of a unified German state. Frederick William IV had also been forced to accept a constitutional regime and to agree that Prussia might be "merged in" Germany. In the middle of May the assembly convened at Frankfurt; it was composed of representatives from all of the German states, including six from the Habsburg Empire. Archduke John of Austria was chosen as the head of the executive branch of the provisional government set up by the assembly. The diet of the Germanic Confederation was declared suspended.

Once the assembly opened, the opposing interests of Prussia and Austria were soon apparent. One of the chief issues of debate was the question of the boundaries of the future united Germany— whether they should include the Austrian-German areas or only the German states. The first alternative, the *grossdeutsch* solution, would preserve Austrian influence in Germany; the second, the *kleindeutsch*, would give Prussia, as the strongest purely German state, a predominant position. The debates extended over many months. During this period the assembly became involved in a complicated controversy over Schleswig-Holstein, which greatly embittered its relations with the great powers and weakened its own position. In March 1849, as has been mentioned, the Austrian government issued a constitution providing for a highly centralized regime. Schwarzenberg then attempted to secure the inclusion of this unitary state in the new German organization. Although there was certainly much attraction in the idea of the creation of a great German-led empire of seventy million inhabitants, this move was obviously too great an upset of the balance between the states in the German area. This union would also not have fulfilled the desire for a purely German national state felt by the representatives at the assembly, who now proceeded to adopt the *kleindeutsch* solution. According to the constitution of March 27, 1849, Germany was to be a federal state, with a parliament of two houses and a hereditary ruler. The German lands of the Habsburg Empire could enter the union when the Austrian constitution was so altered as to allow it.

Having completed its task of organization, the assembly then offered the crown of the new Germany to Frederick William IV. Only a few days later he rejected the office, since it was presented by a popularly elected body. This refusal was a disaster for the assembly, which had no alternate candidate for the position. The attempt to secure the unity of Germany "from below," that is, through a liberal, national, popular movement, thus failed. In April Schwarzenberg recalled the Austrian representatives, and by the end of June the last remnents of the assembly had been dispersed. The question of German unity now lay in the hands of the rulers. Although Frederick William IV would not receive the crown from elected delegates, he labored hard to achieve this same goal through agreement with the German princes.

Prussia's attempt to secure German unity under her leadership came too late. When Austria was involved in Italy and Hungary, Prussia could have used the opportunity to advance her position in the Germanies. The victory in Hungary, however, allowed the Habsburg government to turn its full attention to the German question. The scheme for Prussian Union at first gained the support of Saxony and Hanover, but they soon withdrew, leaving Prussia with the backing of only the smaller German states. In answer to the Prussian moves Schwarzenberg now called for the restoration of the Germanic Confederation. Prussia and Austria thus stood opposed. Prussia retained the allegiance of the small states; the middle powers preferred the Habsburg program, which best protected their independent position. In March 1850 an assembly held at Erfurt, attended by Prussia and her supporters, accepted a Prussian-sponsored constitution. In reply Austria in May held a conference at Frankfurt and reconstituted the Germanic Confederation.

At this point in the controversy the attitude of the great powers assumed significance. Neither Russia, France nor Britain looked with favor on the creation of a truly united German state; all preferred a return to the former loose organization. Therefore the Austrian proposals for the reconstitution of the Germanic Confederation were favored. Only Russia, however, took an active part in the dispute between the two German states. In her relations with Russia Austria had certain decided advantages. Nicholas I had just come to the aid of Austria in Hungary. The tsar at this time also appears to have felt a certain affection and responsibility for the young Francis Joseph. He was angry with Prussia because of that power's attitude in the Schleswig-Holstein controversy and because of what the tsar considered to be Frederick William's compromises with the revolution in Prussia. Schwarzenberg knew well how to handle the tsar and pamper his conservative inclinations. The Habsburg minister now gave the assurance that the Austrian constitution would be abolished.

However Nicholas I acted not so much on the basis of affection or personal inclination as on what were obviously the Russian interests in the central European area. He wished to restore the old balance and to bring Prussia and Austria together to form a front against the revolutionary forces. A minor crisis regarding the state of Hesse-Cassel brought Prussia and Austria to the point of war. At this time, by siding with the Habsburg Empire, Nicholas I made his full influence felt. At a meeting at Olmütz in November 1850 the Prussian king was forced to abandon his entire program of the Prussian Union and to accept the reformation of the Germanic Confederation.

The Austrian victory was nevertheless not complete. Nicholas I had no interest in the establishment of absolute Habsburg predominance in the Germanies. In December 1850 a conference of German states was held at Dresden. Here Prussia and other German governments, with full Russian approval, prevented Schwarzenberg from bringing the entire Austrian empire into the confederation. Central Europe now went back to the organization of 1815. In May 1851 Austria and Prussia resumed their former friendly relations and signed a treaty of mutual assistance.

Although Schwarzenberg thus failed to secure the inclusion of all of the Austrian lands in the confederation, he tried to obtain a similar aim in the economic field. His energetic policies in diplomacy were seconded by those of Karl Ludwig von Bruck in economic matters. It was quite obvious that the Zollverein under Prussian leadership had been a great success. Schwarzenberg and Bruck now wished to bring the Habsburg Empire into an economic union with the German states to create a great tariff-free area from the Adriatic to the North Sea. Once again complicated political maneuvers took place among the German states. Prussia, as could be expected, made great efforts to block the Austrian moves. The death of Schwarzenberg in April 1852 took the main drive out of Austrian diplomacy; Prussia was able to maintain the former arrangements. The empire and the Zollverein made a separate trade treaty.

By 1851 central Europe had thus returned to the general political conditions of the pre-March days. Prussia and Piedmont had constitutional regimes, but the national principle had everywhere been defeated. Under the brilliant leadership of Schwarzenberg, backed by the Habsburg army, the court had suppressed the revolution in its own lands and in Italy, and had reestablished its position in Germany. 1850 marks the last year of victory for the empire. Until this time the Austrian leaders had been able, on the basis of conservative principles, to hold their lands together and to avoid in international relations situations that might endanger their internal or external security. Despite the conflicts with Russia on the Eastern Question and with Prussia over German affairs, they had usually cooperated with the two other conservative courts and had thus been a part of a favorable diplomatic alignment. In 1853 the empire was to face an international situation that placed it in a highly precarious position—and this time there were no Kaunitzes, Metternichs or Schwarzenbergs to invent ingenious solutions to Austria's problems.

Chapter 2

The Crimean War

After the death of Schwarzenberg, whom he admired and held in real affection, the twenty-two-year-old Francis Joseph was determined to make his own decisions in foreign affairs. From this time on, although he allowed his ministers much influence and authority in internal affairs, international relations and military matters became his exclusive province. When the policies of the succeeding foreign ministers are discussed below it must be remembered that the real responsibility for Austrian actions lay in the hands of the emperor. Although he might consult with the various ministers (in fact, crown councils were regularly held to discuss specific issues), he did make the final decisions. His position in foreign affairs thus resembled that of the Russian and Prussian rulers, who also retained control of foreign policy. From this time no Austrian foreign minister enjoyed the position and prestige of either Metternich or Schwarzenberg, and certainly none gained even a semblance of the political power that Bismarck was to hold in Prussia.

Because of his long reign, from 1848 to 1916, the basic concepts of Francis Joseph are thus of the greatest importance for Austrian foreign policy. There is little indication that his ideas underwent a process of real change in this period. The emperor's youth, like Metternich's, had been overshadowed by revolutionary events. The impressions he gained then, and later under the influence of his first adviser, Schwarzenberg, appear to have remained with him throughout his life. In 1848 Francis Joseph had seen his state almost split asunder by the forces of liberalism and nationalism. He thereafter felt little understanding for or sympathy with either of these two profound forces of his day. Nationalism in its many forms remained throughout his reign the chief threat to his country and his dynasty. In international relations his ideas were much akin to those of Metternich. He believed in the preservation of the European balance and the status quo of 1815. In German affairs, again like Metternich, he wished Austria and Prussia to cooperate; after the unification of Germany in 1870 he was a firm supporter of the alliance of the two countries. His chief aim in foreign policy was the protection of the Austrian position as a great power and the maintenance of her territories intact. Since to him the state and the dynasty were identical conceptions, he felt it a matter of personal honor not to surrender any land unless he had been defeated in a war. He held strongly to the sanctity of international treaties and to legality in international relations.

As a person he possessed the virtues of a prince of the old regime; he was honorable, tactful, courteous, and he showed great bravery in the Italian war of 1859. He learned self-discipline as a youth, and he had a real capacity for hard work. He had little interest in the arts or in general ideas or new concepts. His mind was practical, not theoretical. However, he loved the natural beauty of the woods and mountains of his country; his only true recreation was hunting. His family life was to contain much tragedy, including his estrangement from and the assassination of his wife, the suicide of his son and, finally, the death of the heir to the throne in 1914. The series of setbacks he was to meet in foreign and domestic affairs was thus paralleled in his personal life.

Schwarzenberg was followed in office by a minister of his choice—Karl Ferdinand von Buol-Schauenstein. An experienced diplomat, Buol had served in London and St. Petersburg, but without particular distinction. A representative of the old diplomatic methods, he was stiff and formal in his manner, but weak in powers of decision. His career was to be marked by a series of disasters in foreign policy. One of the first problems he had to face concerned relations with France. In December 1852 Louis Napoleon overthrew the republic, proclaimed the Second Empire and adopted the title Napoleon III. The change in the European attitude toward Napoleonic France is best indicated by the fact that diplomatic negotiations now centered not on the quesion of the danger of the revival of French aggression under a new Bonaparte but on how this self-appointed emperor should be addressed. The British government recognized the new title at once; the three Eastern monarchies could not so easily agree. Buol proposed to the tsar that instead of the regular address "Mon frère," the word "Sire" be used. Nicholas I countered with the suggestion "Sire et bon ami." Finally, Prussia and Austria accepted "Mon frère," but the tsar continued his attempt to maintain the dignity of the legitimate monarchs. For Austria the great danger of the accession of another Napoleon was, of course, that the new government would resume an active Italian policy.

However, it was not the Italian peninsula but the Balkans that were to be the next center of diplomatic activity. Although this area had proved usually to be a cause of discord between Vienna and St. Petersburg, Nicholas I continued to lend Austria the type of support he had just given in the Hungarian and German conflicts in the controversy that now arose in Montenegro. At this time, with Austrian approval, the Prince-Bishop of Montenegro, Danilo Petrović, secularized his state. He did not think it was necessary to obtain the approval of the Porte, because he considered himself an independent prince. The Ottoman government did not agree with this interpretation of his position and prepared to fight. The Habsburg Empire, fearing the effect of such a war on the Slavic peoples in the Balkans and in their own lands, and also a possible Russian intervention, sent an ultimatum to the Porte to withdraw from Montenegro. Nicholas I, who was far more sympathetic to Montenegro than Austria was, naturally approved the Habsburg course of action. The tsar sent Francis Joseph a letter expressing full support:

> "I do not know what Thy decisions may be, but whatever they are, if war by Turkey against Thee should result, Thou mayest be assured in advance that it will be precisely the same as though Turkey had declared war on myself."[12]

Thus, Russia once again lent her support to Austrian policy, although of course this action was also in the Russian interest.

---

[12] Joseph Redlich, *Emperor Francis Joseph of Austria* (New York: MacMillan, 1929), pp. 127–28.

Meanwhile a crisis was developing in Constantinople over the conflicting claims of the Orthodox and Catholic churches over the Holy Places in Palestine. Within the Ottoman Empire France was recognized as the chief spokesman for the Catholic church; Russia claimed a similar position in regard to the Orthodox. During the French Revolution and in the years thereafter the Catholic position in the Holy Places had suffered, while the Orthodox had made gains. After 1840 interest in France in the Holy Places revived, and the Catholics pressed their government to win back what had been lost. The French thus exerted pressure on the Porte, and in December 1852 the Ottoman government made a decision in favor of the French. Nicholas I reacted immediately with strong measures; in February 1853 he sent Prince A. S. Menshikov to Constantinople with the aim of protecting Orthodox interests and of reasserting Russian influence in the Ottoman Empire. Menshikov, a brusk and tactless diplomat, not only discussed the question of the Holy Places but made demands that amounted to Ottoman recognition of Russia as the protector of the Orthodox subjects of the sultan. A compromise was soon reached on the question of the Holy Places, but the Ottoman Empire could not allow another power such far-reaching rights concerning its internal affairs. The British ambassador, Lord Stratford de Redcliffe, used his influence to bolster the confidence of the Ottoman government in its resistance to Russian pressure. At the end of May Menshikov left Constantinople; ten days later the Russian government issued an ultimatum stating that if the Porte did not accept its demands it would occupy the Danubian Principalities. In June the British and French fleets moved to Besika Bay, within easy sailing distance of the Turkish capital. In July the Russian armies occupied the Principalities.

With the Russian forces poised on the Danube and the French and British navies near Constantinople, the attention of both sides in the conflict now turned to central Europe, particularly to Austria. If a war should take place, the attitude of the Austrian government was of vital importance to all the powers involved. From the beginning of the crisis, and in Eastern matters in general, Nicholas I appears to have taken Austrian support for granted. He believed that Austrian and Russian interests were identical and that he could count on the Habsburg government to feel a sense of obligation for the services Russia had rendered in 1849. Here the tsar made a grave miscalculation. The point of weakness in the Holy Alliance had always been the Eastern Question. Austria could come to an agreement with Russia only when that power supported the status quo. In 1853 Russia was instead attempting to extend her influence; again the danger had arisen that a Russo-Turkish war might end in the dissolution of the Ottoman Empire. Russian aid to Austria in the past years had not changed the basic Habsburg interests in the Balkans.

Throughout the entire period of the Crimean War Austria was faced with a virtually impossible situation. Almost every course of action open to her was filled with potential danger. Russia was her ally in the Holy Alliance; this power felt strongly about the necessity of the suppression of revolutionary agitation in Europe. She was thus a strong support to the Habsburg conservative political policies. Yet Austria could not afford to allow a major Russian victory in the Balkans because of the effect it might have on the balance of power and on her own Slavic people. The Russian occupation of the Principalities was also looked upon with great disfavor. Austria feared that Russia might remain permanently in the area, an action that would give St. Petersburg further military and strategic advantages against the monarchy and endanger the freedom of Austrian communications on the Danube. Moreover, open cooperation with Russia was not feasible because of the possible repercussions in Italy. The French government throughout this period always used the threat of action in Italy to put pressure on Vienna. It was now clear that Piedmont would take action if assured of French backing.

While close support of Russia was thus excluded, alliance with the Western powers presented grave problems. It was quite clear that if war came and if Austria joined these states, the main strength of the Russian military effort would be directed against the Habsburg Empire. The position of Prussia would then be decisive. It was not logical to contemplate war with Russia without prior assurance of Prussian support. Yet Russophile tendencies were strong in Berlin; it was clear that Frederick William IV would not fight Nicholas I. Moreover, the danger always existed that Prussia would use the Austrian embarrassment in the Eastern Question to strengthen her position in Germany.

Throughout the Crimean crisis Vienna remained the center of diplomatic negotiations. Austria was indeed placed in an unfortunate position, and the entire affair was not handled with wisdom. One of the major difficulties was the division of opinion within the Austrian government. The military leaders, particularly Radetzky and Windischgrätz, feared a war with Russia. They saw the great dangers of engaging in a land battle with the Russian armies. In contrast many of the most prominent diplomats, including Buol, the minister of interior, Alexander von Bach, and the ambassadors in Frankfurt and Paris, Anton von Prokesch-Osten and Alexander von Hübner, strongly supported maintaining ties with the West. There was general agreement only on the proposition that Russia must not be allowed to dominate the Balkans. Francis Joseph, caught between the two conflicting currents, was chiefly concerned with preserving all of his territories. It appeared that his Austrian possessions were in no danger from Russia, whereas his Italian lands were threatened by French action. The French pressure thus worked; Austrian policy tended to swing more to the Western side. However, no clear decisions were ever made and no single policy was adhered to. The fear of Prussian action in Germany, the Russian moves into the Balkans and the French threat to Italy paralyzed the Austrian statesmen.

The summer of 1853 was a period of great diplomatic activity, with the center in Vienna. Here the French ambassador, E. Drouyn de Lhuys, formulated the Vienna Note, with the cooperation of Buol and the other ambassadors. This attempt to mediate between the Russian and Ottoman governments failed largely because at this time the Porte was less interested in seeking a peaceful solution to the conflict. It felt that it had the backing of France and Britain, and it was now willing to enter into a new test of strength with its historic enemy. The Russians were also confident that their Holy Alliance partners would at least remain neutral if war broke out.

Meanwhile the crisis deepened. On September 23 the British government ordered the Mediterranean fleet to Constantinople; this action heartened the Ottoman government, which on October 4 declared war on Russia. In the next weeks the Ottoman troops crossed the Danube into Wallachian territory, and on November 30 a Russian fleet annihilated a Turkish squadron at the battle of Sinope. Diplomatic relations with the Western powers continued to deteriorate, but it was not until March 28, 1854, that the British and French governments finally declared war on Russia.

With the entrance of the two Western powers into the conflict the position of Austria became even more difficult. Pressure was renewed from both sides. The great problem facing France and Britain was how they could come in contact with and defeat Russia. In the Near East the allies had chiefly sea power; Russia was a land power. The Western belligerents' best approach to their enemy was through Austrian territory, and the most convenient instrument with which to deal with Russia was the Austrian army. The Russian government, of course, was well aware of this danger. Throughout the war it asked at the most for armed neutrality from Prussia and Austria. If this doorway to its territories were kept closed, the Russian government could hope to win the war. If Austria and Prussia were to join the West, Nicholas I would face a major disaster, for Russia could not withstand a coalition of the European powers. Although Russia was able to secure assurances of Prussian neutrality, the position of Austria always remained in doubt. Russia tried to gain Austrian neutrality by a promise that no changes would be made in the Balkans without the consent of the monarchy; Austria wanted the assurance that the status quo would be maintained, a condition to which Russia, engaged in a costly war, could not agree.

Although the Austrian and Prussian attitudes toward St. Petersburg differed in many respects, it was to the interest of both powers to keep the war out of central Europe. In April 1854 they signed a pact in which they guaranteed each other's territorial possessions and agreed to go to war if Russia crossed the Balkan Mountains. Other German states also adhered to this understanding. Austria thus had on paper the support of Prussia for her Italian possessions. With this treaty behind her, Austria now turned to Russia. In June an ultimatum was delivered to St. Petersburg to withdraw from the Danubian Principalities. After the Russian government had complied, the monarchy made an agreement with the Ottoman Empire and occupied the provinces itself. These Austrian moves against Russia were accompanied by a mobilization of the army. This action forced Russia to concentrate more troops on the Habsburg borders, which diminished the number available for action against the Western allies.

After having made an agreement with the German states and having forced Russia out of the Principalities, Austria turned to the Western powers and attempted with them to find a way to end the war. In August the allies and Austria issued the Vienna Four Points, which were to become eventually the basis for peace. These conditions included removal of the Russian protectorate over Serbia and the Principalities, provisions for guaranteeing the freedom of navigation of the Danube, revision of the regulations concerning the Straits and establishment of a great-power guarantee over the Christian subjects of the Ottoman Empire to replace the Russian claims to an exclusive protectorate. Since the war had not yet been lost on the battlefield, the Russian government naturally refused to accept these stipulations.

In September 1854 the Western powers commenced an attack on Russian soil with the invasion of the Crimea. The pressure on Vienna was simultaneously increased. In December 1854 the Austrian government signed an alliance with the Western allies, which included a guarantee of its territories for the period of the war. Mobilization was completed, but war was not declared on Russia. In January 1855, in a move directed against the Habsburg Empire, the allies brought Piedmont into the war. In March Nicholas I died and was succeeded by Alexander II, on whose shoulders fell the unhappy task of overseeing the final defeat of the Russian army in the Crimea and of concluding a peace detrimental to Russian interests.

The capture in September 1855 of Sebastopol, the chief Russian strong point in the Crimea, was the last major military action of France and Britain. In November the Russians took Kars from the Turks, but this victory did not compensate for their losses elsewhere. Negotiations had continued throughout the fighting. The allied demands had now risen. The British hoped to obtain the neutralization of the Black Sea; Austria wished Russia to be compelled to surrender part of her Bessarabian lands and the mouth of the Danube. In December 1855 Austria finally took a decisive step. She delivered an ultimatum to St. Petersburg that she would enter the war if peace were not made on the basis of the Vienna Four Points with the additional conditions mentioned above. Unable to resist this combination of powers, the Russian government agreed to the terms.

Although Austria did thus join the allies, her actions in the previous months had alienated her from all of the states. The Russian reaction could be expected. It appeared that the Habsburg government had repaid the Russian aid of 1849 with a rank betrayal. The occupation of the Principalities and the final ultimatum were particularly resented. The Russian ambassador to Vienna at this time was Alexander Gorchakov, who was to become Russian foreign minister. Throughout his career he remembered the Austrian action and the danger in which it had placed his nation. France and Britain were also not content with Habsburg policy. At the peace conference the

Austrian government was made to feel the hostility of the other powers.

The conference opened in Paris on February 25, 1856, and a final treaty was signed on March 30. The meeting was attended by the belligerent powers—Russia, France, Britain, the Ottoman Empire, Sardinia and Austria. British opposition to Prussia, because of her consistently neutral attitude in the war, meant that this power was allowed to attend only the sessions on the Straits. Since the basis of the peace had already been agreed upon, the principal negotiations concerned the application and interpretation of the Vienna Four Points with the additional provisions. The British were concerned chiefly with gaining the neutralization of the Black Sea. This provision was the most important part of the final settlement and the source of the deepest discomfort and humiliation to Russia. The Habsburg Empire was more interested in the status of the Danube River. In the conference Buol was able to secure the cession by Russia of the three southern districts of Bessarabia and to see the mouth of the Danube returned to Turkish control. The Danube River was now put under an international commission, of which Russia was not a member since she was no longer a riverain state. The removal of Russian influence from the Principalities and from the shores of the Danube was the Habsburg Empire's major achievement at the conference. Russia was also forced to give up Kars and to abandon her protectorate of Serbia and the Danubian Principalities. These provinces and the Christian population of Turkey were put under the joint custody of the powers.

The conference dealt, in addition, with the Rumanian and Italian questions. Cavour was allowed to speak on the conditions in Italy and to denounce Austrian influence in the peninsula. The question of the status of the Danubian Principalities was the subject of a more involved debate. Buol evidently had some hopes of maintaining Habsburg paramount influence in the provinces, which were still occupied by Austrian forces, but at the conference he received absolutely no support for this idea. Instead, Napoleon III made himself the spokesman for the national interests of this Latin nation as well as for Italy. He now came out in favor of what had been the program of the Rumanian revolutionary party in 1848—the union of the Principalities and the appointment of a foreign prince. Because this arrangement would further diminish Turkish rights in the area, both the Ottoman Empire and Austria strongly opposed it. The

British government, too, finally decided that it did not wish to see a weakening of Ottoman influence here. However, since no clear agreement could be reached on Rumanian affairs at the conference, the powers decided to refer the matter to a commission.

For Austrian foreign policy the Crimean War had perhaps more significant consequences than any other single event in the nineteenth century. Most important for the future was the change in the Russian position in international relations. As we have seen, both Alexander I and Nicholas I had been ardent advocates of the maintenance of the territorial status quo and the preservation of conservative government in Europe. The Russian rulers had been willing to back their political convictions with military force, and they had always played an active role in European affairs. The Crimean defeat brought about an almost complete reversal of these policies. Recognizing that a reform in their internal structure was essential, the Russian statesmen now adopted the policy of *recueillement,* which signified that they intended to turn their prime attention inward, to internal affairs rather than to foreign policy. Equally important, it now became clear that Russia would not under all circumstances uphold the status quo in Europe. In the years after the Congress of Paris the first aim of Russian policy became the destruction of the treaty of 1856, especially the Black Sea clauses and those pertaining to southern Bessarabia. Russia was thus no longer the firm supporter of the treaty structure of Europe or of legality in international relations. She too wished to tear up a treaty. This change of attitude directly affected Austria, but even more significant was the real animosity that Russia now felt toward Vienna. The Russian statesmen, in particular the new foreign minister, Alexander Gorchakov blamed Austria for having contributed the largest share in forcing Russia to accept a damaging peace. Any similar humiliations inflicted upon Austria in the future were thus bound to be greeted with joy in St. Petersburg.

Despite the fact that Austria had finally joined the Western allies at the end of the war, no real advantages were gained from this action for future diplomatic activity. In April 1856 Austria, Britain and France signed a secret treaty designed to uphold the settlement. By this time, however, it was already clear that the war coalition would not hold together. In the next years not only was Austria to be divided from France, but also France was to be separated from Britain. Instead a new combination, that of Russia and France, began to play a leading role in international relations, at least in the years immediately following the Crimean War. As a result Austria found herself, for all practical purposes, isolated. The Holy Alliance had ceased to exist; an alignment with Prussia alone was not a reliable support because of the conflicting interests of the two powers in the German area. Britain, without a land army, could not play a deciding role in continental affairs, even if she had wished to support Austrian policies. To deepen further the Austrian difficulties, the Habsburg ministers were soon to find themselves confronted with a trio of brilliant and adventurous statesmen—Napoleon III, Cavour and Bismarck—all of whom wished to put through programs that could be carried out only at the expense of the monarchy. Moreover, none of these men were traditional, old-style diplomats; all were willing to use virtually any means to attain their ends, and they could use the revolutionary concepts of the day in one form or another to further their own plans. When confronted by these men the Austrian diplomats were to show that they could not play the game according to the new rules.

For the future course of Austrian foreign policy the plans and character of Napoleon III were most significant, since he gave the impetus to the initiation of the great national unification movements of this period. A strong supporter of the national principle, he favored the redrawing of the map of Europe along these lines. The settlement of 1815 had marked a French defeat; the heir of Napoleon I could now redeem French national honor and reestablish Paris as the diplomatic center of Europe. The French emperor also always expected to win concrete territorial compensation for France from any new arrangement of boundaries. His interest centered on four national movements—those in Hungary, Poland, Italy and the Danubian Principalities. Since he needed Russian support he did not dare act in the Polish question. However he was able to intervene effectively, first, in Rumanian affairs and, second, in the Italian peninsula. In both instances the power whose interests were directly injured was the Habsburg Monarchy. The Austrian statesmen now found themselves faced, in areas of vital concern, with the active opposition of a great power and one that could make full use of the revolutionary conceptions of liberalism and nationalism to further its own foreign-policy goals.

Chapter 3

The Unification of the Danubian Principalities and Italy

The Union of Moldavia and Wallachia   The first victory of the national principle after the Crimean War occurred in the Danubian Principalities. In March 1857 the Austrian occupying forces were withdrawn from the provinces in accordance with the agreement reached in Paris in 1856. Since it could not hope to dominate the area itself, the Habsburg government wished to assure the restoration of Ottoman control and to hinder the advance of the national movement. In fact, Austria now became a stronger defender of Ottoman rights than the Turks themselves. Within the Principalities Austria also had certain advantages. In Moldavia her policies were supported by some members of the great aristocratic families who were not sympathetic with the liberal ideas of those who wished the establishment of a Rumanian national state.

However, the real political strength in the Principalities lay in the hands of the national forces. Their program remained the unification of the Principalities, the appointment of a foreign prince and, eventually, the winning of complete independence from Ottoman control. At the Congress of Paris in 1856 the first two aims had been warmly endorsed by Napoleon III, with the backing of Russia. The Porte and Austria opposed them. The pivotal position was thus held by Britain, who at first supported Ottoman interests. At Paris it was finally decided that, since no agreement could be reached among the powers, the wishes of the Rumanian people would be determined before a final settlement was made. Obviously fraudulent elections, held in July 1857, resulted in a vote against union and a severe straining of French-British relations. In August 1857 the Rumanian problem was discussed at a meeting at Osborne between Napoleon III, Queen Victoria and their foreign ministers. Here it was agreed that another election would be held; Napoleon III abandoned his insistence upon unification. The new election, held in September 1857, led to the formation of an assembly whose members promptly voted the unionist program. The powers once again intervened. In August they signed a convention in which some concessions were made to unionist sentiments, but the separation of the Principalities was reaffirmed. The Rumanian electorate nullified this provision by simply electing Alexander Cuza as governor in both provinces. Another period of international tension followed. Austria and the Ottoman Empire remained the chief opponents of Rumanian national unification; France, with Russian acquiescence, supported it. Austrian opposition was, however, paralyzed by the outbreak of war with Piedmont in the spring of 1859. The Habsburg government was thus not able to obtain the annulment of the double election of Cuza, nor was it able to prevent the amalgamation of the administrative and legislative systems of the two provinces that was accomplished in 1861. In 1866 the second part of the program of the nationalists, the election of a foreign prince, was carried through. At that time Cuza was overthrown and Prince Charles of Hohenzollern-Sigmaringen replaced him. Austria, deeply involved in the conflict with Prussia, was again unable to act.

The establishment of this Rumanian state, limited to the provinces of Moldavia and Wallachia, was, of course, not a direct and immediate threat to the empire, unless it made an alliance with a Habsburg opponent. The danger for Austria lay in what would probably be the future course of the Rumanian national movement. In Transylvania and Bukovina the Habsburg Empire controlled lands that were in the majority Rumanian in population. At the time the Rumanians here were mostly a peasant people who lived in a position of marked political subservience to the other nationalities of the province. It could be expected that in the future they would be drawn increasingly toward the Rumanian state, particularly if their political status in the Habsburg lands failed to improve.

UNIFICATION OF ITALY

MILES	0	50	100	150

TUSCANY	Independent states in 1815
- - - - - - -	Northern boundary of Kingdom of Italy, 1866-1919
1859	Joined by plebiscite with Sardinia
1860	Joined by revolution and plebiscite with Sardinia, to form Kingdom of Italy, proclaimed 1861
1866, 1870	Joined with Kingdom of Italy

From Bryce Lyon, Herbert Rowen, and Theodore S. Hamerow, *A History of the Western World* (Chicago: Rand McNally & Company, 1969), p. 655. Cartography by Willis R. Heath.

The Unification of Italy   Although the formation of a unified Rumania was viewed as a disadvantage for Austria, the act had involved no loss of territory or prestige for the monarchy. Quite the opposite was the case in Italy, where Austria had to fear for both her possession of Lombardy-Venetia and her influence in the peninsula. After the failure of the revolutions of 1848–1849 the Habsburg position had again been strong. Treaties linked Tuscany, Parma, Modena and the Kingdom of the Two Sicilies to Austria; Habsburg troops occupied a part of the Papal States. Despite these diplomatic and military successes, Austrian predominance was opposed by ever-widening circles of the population. The monarchy was blamed for the continuation of the bad government of the Papal States and the Kingdom of the Two Sicilies. A sincere attempt was made to introduce a good administrative system into Lombardy-Venetia, but most of the inhabitants would have preferred a less efficient and purely Italian rule.

Piedmont continued to be the only Italian state that had managed to remain free of Habsburg influence. In 1852 Camillo di Cavour became premier. A practical politician who knew how to exploit the opportunities that came his way, Cavour adopted a program aimed at the establishment of Piedmontese leadership in Italy. He first undertook internal reforms to make Piedmont a model state that would attract the support of other Italians. Relations with Austria soon became very strained. In 1853 an uprising in Milan won much sympathy in Piedmont. After the rebellion had been put down the Austrian government sequestered the property of the participants, some of whom were Piedmontese citizens. This action, together with a bitter press campaign in Piedmont, resulted in a further strain on the diplomatic relations of the two states. Cavour's role in the Crimean War and at the Congress of Paris has already been mentioned. It became apparent at that time that Napoleon III would give at the very least diplomatic support to Piedmont. In fact, the French emperor placed Italian interests much before those of the Danubian Principalities in the diplomatic negotiations of the period. One of his solutions for the Italian question was the exchange by Austria of the possession of Lombardy-Venetia for Moldavia and Wallachia.

Cavour, like Bismarck, was an intensely realistic statesman. He understood the lessons of 1848: Piedmont could not win alone. The support of a great power was essential. After the Crimean War only two sources of possible aid existed: France and Britain. Cavour would have preferred cooperation with Britain, but he needed the assistance of a state with an army that could be used against Austria. He fully understood the danger that might come from France in the form of a demand for compensation or the establishment of French domination in Italy. Nevertheless he proceeded to make great efforts to win Napoleon III to the Piedmontese cause. The task was not easy. Cavour was probably aided by the attempt made on Napoleon's life in January 1858 by an Italian revolutionary, Orsini. The French emperor was greatly shaken by the event; from prison Orsini directed strongly emotional appeals to him to free Italy. Secret negotiations were carried on subsequently between agents of Cavour and Napoleon III, who acted behind the back of the French foreign minister, Walewski.

Finally, in July 1858 Napoleon III and Cavour met at Plombières to agree on a plan of action against Austria. Here Napoleon promised to aid Piedmont in a war against her northern neighbor, but on the condition that a good pretext be found and that revolutionary means not be employed. It should be noted that at this time Napoleon did not favor the establishment of a unitary Italian nation. He wished instead that Italy would remain divided into satellite states that would look to France for leadership. The Plombières agreement provided for the reconstruction of Italy into four divisions—first, a kingdom of northern Italy under the house of Savoy, including Piedmont, Venetia, Lombardy, Parma, Modena and part of the Papal territories; second, the city of Rome and the surrounding lands, which would remain under the pope; third, a kingdom of central Italy with Tuscany and the rest of the papal possessions; and fourth, the Kingdom of the Two Sicilies. These new states were to be organized into a confederation with the pope as president. As compensation France was to gain the provinces of Nice and Savoy, which belonged to Piedmont. In December a formal treaty of alliance was signed providing for war against Austria.

After the agreement had been concluded, Cavour's main task was to promote a war with Austria in which the monarchy would appear as the clear aggressor. In the meantime Napoleon III continued to prepare the diplomatic background for future action. The chief French problem was to secure the cooperation of Russia. The Russian government showed itself quite willing to allow a humiliation of Austria, but it would not accept a real reduction in the position of the state as a great power. In a treaty of March 1859 Russia agreed only to maintain an attitude of benevolent neutrality and to attempt to influence Prussia and the German states to adopt a similar attitude if war broke out. Napoleon was not able to get the wider alliance he would have preferred.

The French-Piedmontese cooperation was perfectly apparent to the Austrian government. During this entire period the Piedmontese press continued violent attacks on Austrian rule in Italy. The problem for the Austrian government was still how to deal with this provocative attitude of Piedmont, backed by France. The British government, chiefly concerned that France not replace Austria as the predominant power in Italy, tried to arrange some sort of mediation. Russia, seconded by France, proposed a European congress. The idea of an international conference was bound to meet with an unenthusiastic reception in Vienna, since it could have no object other than the removal or limitation of Austrian control in Italy.

Austria meanwhile attempted to win the assistance of Prussia. Archduke Albrecht was sent to Berlin to try to arrange a basis of cooperation. The Prussian government, however, was divided. In October 1858 Prince William became regent; Frederick William IV was no longer capable of governing the state. Prince William favored a policy of cooperation with Britain, but he could not completely abandon Vienna. In Prussia, Austria was regarded as a fellow German state, and German liberals in general were concerned with her fate. The Prussian government was also aware that the Austrian difficulties could be used to further Prussian interests in the German area. It was this last consideration that was to predominate during the Italian crisis. Prussia now demanded a partition of the armed forces of the Germanic Confederation with herself in command in northern Germany. Austria was not prepared to concede her leadership in Germany to protect her preponderance in Italy.

By this time the tension between Piedmont and Austria had heightened. Cavour was never certain that Napoleon III would indeed honor his agreement; the Piedmontese minister therefore further increased his provocative policies toward the Habsburg Empire in order to try to bring about a war before the French emperor changed his mind. In March he mobilized the Piedmontese army, declaring that this act was in answer to similar moves by Austria. He also established a corps in his army made up of refugees from Lombardy. The Austrian government reacted to these actions exactly as Cavour wished. On April 23 it delivered an ultimatum with a three-day time limit demanding that Piedmont demobilize. Cavour now had what he wanted. The Austrian demands were rejected; at the end of April Habsburg armies invaded Piedmont, thus bringing into effect the French-Piedmontese agreement.

The Austrian action had been based on a complete miscalculation of the European diplomatic situation. It was evidently believed that France would restrain Piedmont, and that even if war came, Britain and Prussia would be sympathetic to the Austrian position. Russian neutrality was assumed because of the past hostility of St. Petersburg to revolutionary national movements. Instead Austria now found herself at war with both Piedmont and France; she was not only without allies, but the attitude of the other European powers was extremely dubious. After the ultimatum had been delivered, Buol had resigned and was replaced by Johann Bernhard von Rechberg. The new minister, who had served under Metternich, was conservative in his views and, like Buol, was never in a strong position in the government. Francis Joseph, in this crucial period of Austrian history, was strongly influenced by the advice of Anton von Schmerling and Ludwig von Biegeleben, the counselor for German affairs in the Austrian foreign office.

During the war the Austrian military leadership proved as incompetent as the diplomacy that had preceded it. General Gyulai, in command in northern Italy, was unequal to his task. Francis Joseph at this time went into the battlefield, where he showed personal bravery but no real talent as a military commander. The Austrian military plans were hampered by the fact that little reliance could be placed on the Italian and Hungarian troops in the army. The unrest in Hungary at this time and the presence of Russian troops on the Galician border also meant that the Austrian army could not concentrate its entire strength on the Italian battlefields.

Certainly one of the greatest disappointments to the Habsburg government was the attitude of Prussia and the Germanic Confederation. Although German public opinion manifested sympathy for the Austrian position, the German states, largely because of the Prussian stand, were unable to offer practical assistance. Prussia still demanded concessions that would have signified a great increase in her power in Germany. Moreover, both Russian and Britain endeavored to keep the German powers neutral. In June Lord Palmerston, with Russell as his foreign minister, was again at the head of the British government. As in 1848 Palmerston wanted Austria out of Italy, but he did not wish to see the monarchy's status as a great power compromised. Russell was a strong supporter of Italian nationalism; both he and Palmerston desired to keep the war localized in the Italian peninsula and not spread to the Rhine.

The war in Italy lasted about three months. Although the Austrians suffered the major defeats, the French army proved only slightly superior in military capabilities. While the fighting was continuing the Piedmontese used the opportunity to stir up revolts in Parma, Modena and Tuscany. In June the French won the two battles of Magenta and Solferino. Despite the fact that his armies were victorious in individual engagements, Napoleon III was not satisfied with the progress of events. He had no desire to see the unification of the peninsula under Piedmont, and he did not like the Piedmontese use of revolutionary means in the Italian states. The military situation also disquieted him. Austria still occupied a strong strategic and military position; the fortresses of the Quadrilateral were not conquered. A real effort would still be required to dislodge Austria from northern Italy; meanwhile the international scene might change to the French disadvantage. Napoleon III was particularly disturbed by events in Germany. In June the Prussian army was finally mobilized; it was not clear how Prussia and the Germanic Confederation would act in the future. Napoleon III could not fight on two fronts. The British and Russian governments were also urging a settlement.

Faced with defeat on the battlefield, the Austrian government too desired peace. In July Francis Joseph and Napoleon III met at Villafranca and arranged the terms to end the war. It was now agreed that Austria would surrender Lombardy to France, who would give it to Piedmont. The monarchy was to retain Venetia and the fortresses of the Quadrilateral. The rulers who had been dispossessed during the war were to be restored. A confederation of Italian states was to be set up in which Austria would continue to exert much influence through her possession of Venetia and her influence with the governments of the Kingdom of the Two Sicilies and the Papal States. This agreement was a bargain between the two rulers; it left them with a division of influence in the peninsula. Both Piedmont and Britain reacted unfavorably to these proposals. Cavour resigned in despair, feeling betrayed by France. From this time on

Britain was to follow a policy of favoring the establishment of an independent and united Italy strong enough to withstand French and Austrian pressure.

Despite the Austro-French agreement the process of Italian unification continued. In this second phase the policies of France and Britain held the center of the stage. Once her armies were defeated Austria could do little to influence the final events. Britain, with her preponderant naval power in the Mediterranean, was in a much better position to act decisively. The chief British concern was still that a national state that would be a French satellite might be established in the peninsula. At one time Britain had agreed to Habsburg predominance in the area because Austria, without a large fleet, could not threaten British interests in the Mediterranean and could be a factor in maintaining the balance of power. France, in contrast, was in active competition with Britain for control of the Mediterranean. Britain now hoped that a united Italy might be created that would be strong enough to resist French pressure.

The immediate problem facing the powers after the peace of Villafranca was the unwillingness of the Italian states who had overthrown their old rulers to receive them back. With strong Piedmontese support, the new regimes stayed in power and proceeded to hold elections for new assemblies. When these bodies met they voted for unification with Piedmont. In January 1860 Cavour returned to office. Napoleon decided to recognize the new events, but he demanded in return the cession of Nice and Savoy, which he had renounced after Villafranca. A series of plebiscites was held in all of the states involved, including Nice and Savoy, and the desired results were obtained. The Austrian government was strongly opposed to these actions, but it recognized that it could not renew hostilities.

The events in the north spurred further action in the south. In April 1860 a revolt broke out in Sicily; in the next month Garibaldi, with the full knowledge of the Piedmontese government, sailed from Genoa with a force of men to assist the rebellion. In the complicated military and diplomatic maneuvering that followed, the Austrian government could play only a small role. Internal problems occupied the full attention of the state. The establishment of a united Italy (including the Kingdom of the Two Sicilies and the Papal States) that now took place involved to a greater extent negotiations between Piedmont, France, Russia and Britain. Of the great powers only Britain benefitted from the formation of the new state. Russia broke off diplomatic relations with Piedmont over the question of the overthrow of the Bourbon ruler of the Kingdom of the Two Sicilies. France had, of course, gained two provinces, but she had also acquired a most troublesome neighbor. Her troops still occupied Rome to protect the pope, whose temporal power was now reduced to the possession of that city. Austrian-Italian friction was similarly not ameliorated. The Italian patriots still had claims against Vienna. They demanded next the cession of Venetia, the south Tyrol and Trieste.

The defeat of the Austrian armies in Italy laid bare the weaknesses not only of the Austrian military establishment but also of the internal structure of the government. For Austria, as for Russia after the Crimean War, a period of internal reform and reorganization was absolutely necessary. Austria had been in a disastrous financial position before the war, and conditions were naturally worse afterward. The military forces and, in particular, the army leadership had been shown too weak to defend the interests of the state. There had also been evidence of corruption in the military administration. As has been mentioned, some of the Hungarian and Italian troops had been judged unreliable.

The main emphasis in the changes made at this time in the Austrian government was toward appeasing the Magyars, who were highly dissatisfied with the centralizing Bach System. In the new constitution, the "October Diploma" of 1860, the Habsburg government was reorganized on a federal basis. The local diets were now given more authority. A central parliament was established, whose deputies were to be chosen by these assemblies. These measures did not satisfy the Magyars, and they were opposed by the German liberals, who preferred a centralized administration. In 1861 another scheme, the February Patent, was introduced. It was chiefly the work of Anton von Schmerling. A return was now made to a unitary system. The power of the local units was reduced, but the central parliament was kept. These changes did not serve to calm internal discontent, which continued throughout the wars of German unification, particularly in Hungary. For Austria the significance of this period of internal reorganization for foreign affairs is clear. The constitutional crises and the constant tension between Vienna and

Budapest weakened the empire in international relations. They had already limited Austrian action in Italian affairs after Villafranca; they were to affect the Austrian ability to handle the Prussian challenge in the next years. In fact, Vienna during this time was compelled to wage a two-front political campaign—against Prussia in Germany and against the Magyars within the empire.

Chapter 4

The Unification of Germany: The Ausgleich

The Habsburg defeat in Italy was followed almost at once by renewed conflicts with Berlin over German affairs. As has been shown,
since the treaty of Vienna the Austrian-Prussian rivalry had been a
constant issue in Habsburg foreign policy. Metternich dealt with
the problem by always holding the initiative in German affairs and
by using the fear of revolution to persuade Frederick William III to
support the maintenance of the conditions of 1815. Schwarzenberg
had used an opposite approach; he had given Frederick William IV
the alternative of fighting or surrendering. Both statesmen, with
different methods, had been successful in preventing changes in the
organization of the German states, which is what they wished to
accomplish. Until the 1860s the Habsburg Empire was thus able
to hold its prime position among the German powers. The middle
states usually supported the Habsburg position. They saw in the
Austro-Prussian dual relationship the best guarantee of their own
existence. They did not want to be absorbed by either power. As
long as particularism rather than nationalism remained the strongest
political motive in the German area, the Habsburg Empire could
hope to maintain its favorable position.

By the middle of the century, however, great economic changes
were underway in Germany. Railroads now linked the major Ger-

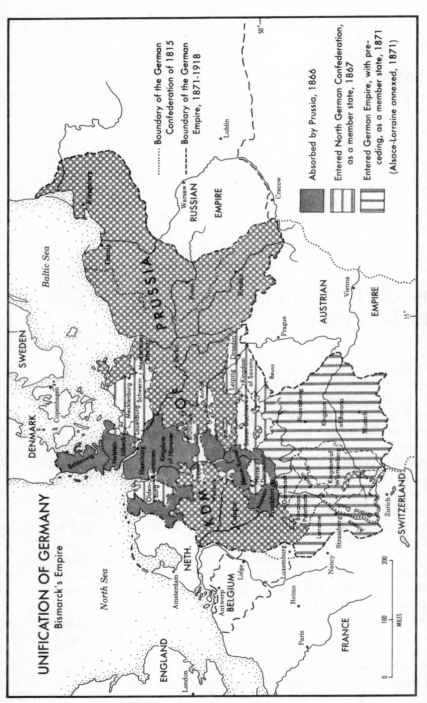

UNIFICATION OF GERMANY
Bismarck's Empire

······· Boundary of the German
      Confederation of 1815
----- Boundary of the German
      Empire, 1871-1918

Absorbed by Prussia, 1866

Entered North German Confederation,
as a member state, 1867

Entered German Empire, with preceding, as a member state, 1871
(Alsace-Lorraine annexed, 1871)

From Bryce Lyon, Herbert Rowen, and Theodore S. Hamerow, *A History of the Western World* (Chicago: Rand McNally & Company, 1969), p. 653. Cartography by Willis R. Heath.

man cities with one another and with the ports of the north. The industrial development that was to make Germany such a strong state after the unification had commenced. Prussian economic leadership had already been demonstrated with the formation of the Zollverein. Moreover, Prussia, with her modern army and good administration, was obviously in all respects far better prepared to lead in German affairs than was the Habsburg Empire, with its multinational character and increasing domestic difficulties. When, after the Italian unification, German nationalism received an added impetus, it became natural that German patriots would look to Prussia, as the Italians had turned to Piedmont, for leadership in the formation of a unified state.

In addition, Prussia herself in these years received the type of leadership necessary to effect great changes in the Germanies. In 1861, after the death of Frederick William IV, William I became the ruler of Prussia. He soon came into conflict with the Prussian parliament over an army bill. As a last resort he appointed as his chief minister Otto von Bismarck, who was believed to be strongly conservative in his outlook. Although Bismarck indeed had little sympathy with liberal ideas as such, he was a man of his times. He understood how to exploit the forces and ideas of his period to gain his own aims in internal and foreign policy. He also already had firm views on Austria. From his experiences as the Prussian representative at the Germanic Confederation he had come to believe that the Habsburg Empire had to be forced out of German affairs. He thus knew from the beginning what he wanted and, like Cavour, he was not overly scrupulous about the means he would use.

Conditions in the Habsburg Empire were quite different. Austria could not claim any particular aptitude in internal administration, her army had just been defeated, and her economic development lagged one step behind that in Germany as a whole. Because of her multinational structure she could not very well take the lead in a purely German national movement. Moreover the Austrian statesmen continued to live in the past; they emphasized the Habsburg role as the preserver of traditions and the defender of the treaty structure of Europe. They were also not in agreement on how Prussia should be treated. Rechberg favored a cautious, conservative policy and cooperation with Berlin. He hoped that Austria and Prussia would come together to oppose the advance of revolutionary concepts in Germany. Schmerling, in contrast, wished Austria to take a strong position, to lead in the reform of the confederation and to maintain her predominance.

The first test of strength between Austria and Prussia in this period came over the question of the Austrian entrance into the Zollverein and the reform of the Germanic Confederation. Each of these issues had been previously a matter of strong debate. In March 1862 Prussia signed a commercial treaty with France that provided for a large reduction in tariffs. At the same time Rechberg proposed that Austria join the Zollverein; he was able to gain the support of the four south German states for this move. As before, Prussia made a determined effort to block the Austrian entrance into the union. In December 1863 Prussia denounced the tariff agreements, which were the basis of the Zollverein, and announced that she would make customs arrangements only with those who would adhere to the Prussian-French treaty. Austria's entrance was precluded because domestic opposition prevented her from lowering her tariffs to the prescribed levels. The German states soon found that they could not afford to remain out of the Prussian-led Zollverein. In 1864 the treaties were renewed on the old conditions. The Zollverein then made a treaty of commerce with the Habsburg Empire in 1865.

The next conflict came over the much discussed question of a reorganization of the Germanic Confederation. In August 1863 Francis Joseph summoned a conference of German princes to discuss the reform of the organization. The proposals presented at this time represented the last Austrian effort to take a position of political leadership in Germany. The meeting was the idea of Francis Joseph, who enjoyed presiding at a congress of German princes. All of the German rulers accepted the invitation except Prussia. With great difficulty Bismarck persuaded William I not to attend. At the meeting the Austrian proposal provided for a tightening of the bonds between the German states with Habsburg predominance clearly preserved. Although a majority of the German rulers, with the king of Saxony at their head, were in favor of the Austrian plan, no reorganization of the confederation could be undertaken without Prussian consent. The Austrian government was thus checked in its attempt both to enter the German customs union and to reform the confederation.

The Austro-Prussian conflict, however, was to be decided not through discussions among the German states but in negotiations among the great powers and, finally, on the battlefield. Here Bismarck could display his great talents as a diplomat and his full understanding of the balance of forces in Europe. It is to his great credit that he realized the importance of securing the support of Russia for any Prussian action in central Europe. After all, it had been Nicholas I who in opting for Francis Joseph had prevented Frederick William IV's attempt to unite Germany previously. Bismarck had been ambassador in St. Petersburg, and he was well regarded in that capital. He was soon able to win even more favor in Russian eyes. In 1863 the second great Polish revolt of the century occurred. Prussia, with a Polish problem of her own, immediately demonstrated her solidarity with and support of the Russian government. Austria, however, again adopted the Crimean position of attempting to stand on both sides while in fact leaning toward the Western powers. Undoubtedly, once again the Austrian statesmen were happy to see Russia embarrassed and also paid back for her attitude in the Italian crisis. They therefore joined with Britain and France in ineffective declarations in favor of the Poles. The Prussian attitude deepened the already friendly dispositions toward Berlin that existed at the time in the Russian court.

The revival of the very complicated Schleswig-Holstein controversy gave Bismarck his first great diplomatic triumph and led to the involvement of Austria in an affair that was to end in another military and diplomatic disaster. The two duchies of Schleswig and Holstein were under the king of Denmark; Holstein was, in addition, a member of the Germanic Confederation, while Schleswig was not. It had been previously apparent that the direct line of the Danish kings was about to die out. According to the Danish law the succession would then pass to Prince Christian of Glücksburg; the duchies, however, which were under the Salic law, would be governed by the Duke of Augustenburg. In 1852 the great powers, most of whom did not wish to see the power of Denmark diminished, agreed in the London Protocol that the duchies would remain with Denmark and the Glücksburg king, but that they would be allowed to keep their separate status. The Augustenburg heir was paid to renounce his claims. In 1863 the Danish government violated the London Protocol by formulating a constitution in which Schleswig was incorporated directly into Denmark. This action infuriated the Germanic Confederation, which had not signed the protocol, and it was decided that federal troops would be sent to occupy Holstein. The crisis was made worse when the Danish king died and was succeeded by Christian IX, who promptly accepted the new constitution. The duchies clearly preferred the Augustenburg candidate; federal troops entered Holstein. Bismarck now moved with skill. The acquisition of the two provinces would be a great advantage for Prussia since they controlled the land route from the Baltic to the North Sea. Kiel was potentially a strong naval base. Prussia thus had something to gain from the situation. The Habsburg Monarchy, in contrast, could make no advances in the area. Annexation of lands in north Germany was obviously not possible. The Austrian aim in acting in the affair was simply to maintain the Habsburg position as the leading German power in an event that had stirred all the Germans. The Habsburg government now called for the reestablishment of the conditions of the London Protocol. The provinces should remain under the Danish king, but their separate status should be respected. Austria thus stood on the treaties, not on German national interests. Since it seemed that Prussian aims were similar, Rechberg favored cooperation with Prussia. In January 1864 the two powers signed a treaty in which they agreed to act together in the question. The exact status of the provinces would be settled later.

In February Austrian and Prussian armies invaded Denmark. The Danes had expected assistance from abroad, especially from the British, but when this did not materialize they could not hope to win. In October, in the Peace of Vienna, they were forced to surrender Schleswig, Holstein and Lauenburg to the victorious allies. The question of the final fate of the duchies still had to be decided. Public opinion in Germany remained strongly against their return to Denmark. The inhabitants themselves would probably have preferred the appointment of an Augustenburg prince and the constitution of the provinces into a separate state within the Germanic Confederation. Bismarck wished to annex them to Prussia, but opinion in his government was divided.

Meanwhile, in October 1864 Rechberg was replaced by Count Alexander von Mensdorff-Pouilly. Because of his own high rank, his marriage to a rich heiress and the fact that he was a cousin of Queen Victoria, the new minister had risen quickly in the diplomatic service. He was known as a good-natured and well-meaning man, but, like his predecessor, he was weak and allowed himself to be influenced by those around him. Biegeleben continued to play the same important role as before. In addition, Count Maurice Esterhazy wielded much influence. Both Mensdorff and Francis Joseph wanted a peaceful settlement of the Danish question. However, in their negotiations with the Prussians a sharper tone was adopted. In August 1865 the administration of the provinces was provisionally provided for in the Convention of Gastein. Here it was agreed that Austria would administer Holstein and Prussia, Schleswig. The territory of Lauenburg was ceded to Prussia for an indemnity. Prussia gained also the harbor of Kiel and the right to build a canal through Holstein. The provinces were to join the Zollverein.

Throughout the Danish crisis the initiative in diplomatic action had remained with Bismarck, and this condition was to continue. The Prussian minister now turned abroad to prepare the diplomatic stage for a test of strength with Austria for the control of Germany. The international situation was quite favorable for an active policy on the part of Prussia. Through the events of the preceding years the former alignments had been dissolved. The Holy Alliance had broken in the Crimean War, and the Franco-British entente no longer existed because of the British government's distrust and fear of Napoleon III. Russia remained opposed to Austria, friendly to Prussia and concerned over France. Britain throughout this period was primarily apprehensive that France would use the opportunity to extend her power to the Rhine or into Belgium. The British and Russian attitudes were thus in the Prussian interest. Austria was isolated. Bismarck's chief diplomatic efforts were now concentrated on negotiations with Napoleon III and Italy. He wished to assure himself of the neutrality of France, and he wanted a war alliance with the new Italian state.

In order to obtain these goals Bismarck met with Napoleon in October 1865 in Biarritz. Here the question of the reorganization of Germany and the problem of Venetia were discussed. In these conversations Bismarck made vague promises of territorial compensation should France remain neutral in an Austro-Prussian war. Napoleon III now completely miscalculated the balance of forces in Europe. Believing that Austria held military superiority, Napoleon III assisted Bismarck in obtaining the Italian alliance that he sought. The French emperor expected to assume the role of arbiter in any conflict that might arise between Vienna and Berlin over Germany and to be able to obtain territorial compensation in the process.

The Prussian military leaders, quite naturally, wanted an agreement with Italy that would force the Habsburg Empire to fight on two fronts. The Italians in turn were happy to have the opportunity to acquire Venetia. The negotiations were protracted because of the Italian distrust of Prussia and the fear that Bismarck might use any alliance simply to force Austria to surrender Schleswig and Holstein. In April 1866 an agreement was finally signed in which the chief advantages lay on the Prussian side. Italy agreed to support Prussia should she go to war with Austria within three months. In return Venetia would be won. The Italian government now strongly wished to precipitate a conflict within the time period allowed. Open preparations were made for war in northern Italy.

Once again the Habsburg government was faced with a situation similar to that of 1859. Prussia and Italy were acting in a deliberately provocative manner. The Austrians felt that they had to take countermeasures, particularly in Italy. In April the command was given to mobilize the southern army; by the end of the month full mobilization was decided upon. The Austrian actions allowed Bismarck to persuade William I to undertake similar military measures. In the beginning of May Prussia also mobilized.

The Austrian government next decided on a course of action that, had it been adopted earlier, might have seriously compromised Bismarck's diplomatic tactics. Recognizing that a war on two fronts was a military impossibility, it was decided that Venetia should be surrendered to Italy with the aim of securing that power's separation from Prussia. Attempts were also to be made to assure French neutrality. Austrian military strength could then be concentrated against Prussia. On June 12 Austria signed a secret treaty with Napoleon III that was unfavorable to Austrian interests. In it Austria obtained the assurance of French neutrality in return for the surrender of Venetia to France no matter what the outcome of a war with Prussia would be. France would then give the province to Italy. If Austria were victorious she would take compensation in Germany, probably in the form of the annexation of Silesia. The Habsburg government further agreed that in the event of victory it would make no major changes in the German area without consultation with France. Thus the Austrian statesmen finally, and too late, abandoned the attempt to hold both their Italian and their German positions and decided to concentrate on the struggle with Prussia. The agreement did not, however, succeed in its principal aim of removing Italy from the war.

Both Austria and Prussia were now diplomatically prepared for conflict. The immediate cause for the outbreak of the war was the

Prussian occupation of Holstein after the- Austrian governor had summoned the diet of the province. Austria then appealed to the diet of the Germanic Confederation, which voted against Prussia, who promptly left the organization. When war finally broke out Austria found most of the middle German states on her side. However, with the exception of Saxony they did not offer effective military support.

From the beginning the war was a military catastrophe for the empire. Successes were gained only in Italy. In June another victory was won at Custozza; in July the Austrian navy defeated the Italians in the battle of Lissa. The decisive engagements, however, occurred not here but on the battlefields of Bohemia. At Königgrätz in July the superior Prussian arms and organization resulted in a great Austrian defeat. The speed and magnitude of the Prussian victories were a distinct shock to the governments of Europe. No one, including Francis Joseph and William I, had expected a quick Prussian triumph. After these successes Bismarck wished to make peace. He had achieved his main purpose; he could now exclude Austria from German affairs. He feared that a prolongation of the conflict would bring about French and Russian intervention.

Although Bismarck and most of the Habsburg statesmen were ready for peace, William I had to be persuaded that it would be dangerous to pursue the war further. The negotiations were complicated because Francis Joseph insisted on standing behind the king of Saxony, his one true ally. He also refused to consider the cession of any Austrian territory except Venetia. In the Preliminary Peace of Nikolsburg in July, terms were finally agreed upon. The most important provision was that Austria would withdraw from Germany and recognize the Prussian right to reorganize the German states north of the river Main. The Germanic Confederation was dissolved, but the south German states, who maintained their independence, could form their own organization. Venetia was at the same time surrendered to Italy and a small indemnity was paid. Thus, after over 600 years of primacy in German affairs, the Habsburg rulers were forced to abandon their historical role in both the German and Italian lands.

The principal result of the war of 1866 was the reorganization of the entire central European area, including the Habsburg Empire. Both the north German states and Austria were placed under new constitutional forms. After the conclusion of the peace, Bismarck proceeded with the direct annexation of Hesse-Cassel, Nassau, Hanover and the city of Frankfurt. He joined the rest of the states north of the river Main into the North German Confederation. The organization given this area is important because it became the basis for the German Empire of 1871. Although a federal form was adopted, in practice Prussia obtained the domination of north Germany. In the new confederation the presidency was held by the king of Prussia; the ministers were responsible to him, and he had effective control of military affairs and foreign policy. The legislative branch was composed of a two-house parliament. The upper house, the *Bundesrat*, was made up of delegates sent by the member states; the lower house, the *Reichstag*, was chosen by universal manhood suffrage, a measure that Bismarck introduced to conciliate German liberal and democratic opinion. The new confederation was linked with the four south German states, which remained outside the organization, by defensive and offensive alliances. The entire German area, of course, remained within the Zollverein. German unification had thus been completed only partially. Austria, the chief supporter of particularism, had been defeated, but the problem of the south German states remained. This question was bound to involve primarily Prussian-French relations.

A similar major change occurred simultaneously in the government of the Habsburg lands. The second defeat of the Austrian army made essential an even more radical transformation of the empire than had occurred after the Italian war. The chief problem remained the Magyar opposition to Habsburg centralist policies. Negotiations between Vienna and Budapest to alter their relations had been underway before the war. In October 1866 Count Frederick Ferdinand von Beust became Francis Joseph's principal adviser and his minister for foreign affairs. Beust, a Saxon, had been regarded as one of the most able of his country's statesmen. His appointment marked the emperor's intention not to accept the decision of 1866 but to continue a policy of opposition to Prussia. Francis Joseph saw the German question as primarily a manifestation of the rivalry of the two houses of Hohenzollern and Habsburg, rather than as a national issue. Thus he now sought to redeem the honor of his family. The aim of Beust's foreign policy in the five years in which he was in office was to be, first, to reform and strengthen the inner structure of the state and, second, to restore to Austria her former status among the great powers.

If Austria was to embark on an active foreign policy, it was obviously first necessary that peace and order should be assured at home. To achieve this aim Beust worked closely with two moderate Hungarian statesmen, Francis Deak and Julius Andrassy. Both of these men wished to obtain virtually complete self-government for Hungary, but not to break the link with Vienna. The final settlement expressed this goal and was a great Magyar political victory. The Ausgleich of 1867 divided the Habsburg Empire into two parts: the kingdom of Hungary and a second division, which had no official name but was referred to as "the lands represented in the Reichsrat." It will henceforth be referred to as Austria. The two divisions were joined by a common ruler and joint ministries of foreign affairs, war and finance. Francis Joseph now became king in Hungary and emperor in Austria. Agreements on tariff, currency, the railroad and the imperial bank were also made, but they had to be renewed periodically. In addition, it was provided that the legislative bodies of Austria and Hungary would each select a delegation of sixty members who would meet together alternately in Vienna and Budapest. Their duty was to approve the budget and to oversee the common ministries.

The Habsburg Empire at this time in fact acquired three governments. In addition to the arrangements made for the state as a whole, each part had its own separate constitutional arrangement. Of the two, Austria received the more liberal regime, although it was one that at first gave the political power to the German minority. The Magyar leaders for their part now proceeded to set up an administrative apparatus in which the entire control of the state was in their hands. In 1868 a special arrangement was made with Croatia-Slavonia, which kept her own diet and the right to use her language in government business. In the next years, however, this agreement was repeatedly infringed upon. Up to 1914 the trend within Hungary was toward the increasing Magyarization of the population of the kingdom.

In the Ausgleich the Magyars and the Germans had a political organization in which they shared the control of the state. Quite naturally this division of political power was opposed by the other nationalities, who would have liked an arrangement similar to that obtained by the Magyars. Of the nationalities within the empire only the Poles, with their virtual control of the administration of Galicia, accepted without great displeasure the new organization. As long as there seemed little hope for the reestablishment of an independent Poland, they preferred to remain with Austria-Hungary rather than seek any other possible political alternative.

Until World War I the nationality problem was to dominate the internal life of the empire and to influence foreign relations directly. The Ausgleich marked the triumph of Magyar nationalism just as much as the unification of Germany and Italy was the victory of the national cause in these areas. The only difference between these movements and that in Hungary was that the Magyar leaders correctly judged that they could not exist as a great power alone. They also wished to hold all of the lands of the Crown of St. Stephen and did not want to run the risk that they might be partitioned along national lines.

The Ausgleich, particularly the strong position that Hungary now held in the combination, was to affect profoundly Habsburg foreign policy. After the Russian intervention of 1849 the Magyar statesmen became and remained Russophobes. In addition, because of their own particular national interests, they were supporters of Prussian predominance in Germany, and they favored strongly the maintenance of the Ottoman Empire. In internal Habsburg affairs they acted to block any reform movement that would allow the other nationalities an equal share in the governing of the country. In 1867 they obtained essentially what they had been struggling for over many years; they now wanted the status quo maintained and protected. The discontent of the Slavic and Rumanian nationalities with this situation weakened the entire empire and complicated Habsburg relations with its neighboring states.

After having played a major part in this internal reorganization, Beust turned his attention to foreign policy. Since he had obtained his aim of excluding the empire from Germany, Bismarck wished to renew friendly relations with Vienna. His chief adversary lay on the other side of the Rhine. The German chancellor, too, did not wish to face a two-front war. Beust, however, was not receptive to a reconciliation. If an anti-Prussian course were to be pursued, he wished a French alignment and an understanding with Italy. Divisions within the Habsburg government, however, hampered his policy. Most important was the opposition of Andrassy. The Magyar statesman had no desire to participate in a possible check to Prussia. There was always a danger that a reversal of 1866 and the return of Habsburg domination in Germany would enable Vienna to undo the Ausgleich.

He therefore argued that Habsburg strength should be conserved to defend the state against Russia and to act in the Balkan area.

In endeavoring to carry out his aims Beust turned to Paris. Here he was favorably received. Napoleon III was at this time no longer the statesman he had been. In this crucial period in French history he was constantly sick and his policy became increasingly irresolute and confused. After the Prussian victory over the empire Napoleon III had immediately sought the compensation to which he felt entitled. Bismarck, now victorious, refused to surrender any German lands. Napoleon III then thought of Belgium and Luxemburg. In 1866 and 1867 he attempted to obtain Luxemburg from its sovereign, the king of Holland. When this plan became known prematurely, Napoleon III was forced to withdraw. After this humiliation he showed himself more eager to form ties with Austria-Hungary. Thereafter, for about two and a half years negotiations dragged on between Vienna and Paris. The Italian government also joined in the discussions. In 1867 Napoleonic policy suffered another setback when Maximilian, the brother of Francis Joseph, was executed in Mexico. In August Napoleon III and his wife paid a visit, ostensibly of condolence, to the Habsburg emperor in Salzburg. Here the common problems of the two governments were discussed, but no agreement was reached.

In negotiating with France the Habsburg government faced certain real difficulties. Despite their desire to prevent Prussia from moving forward again, the Habsburg diplomats could not act too openly against German national interests because of the sentiments of the German liberals in Austria. For the same reason, they could not promise German lands to the French ruler, but Napoleon III always hoped for some sort of territorial compensation. Moreover, the empire needed an alliance that would assist it in the Balkans and against Russia if necessary. France would not offer aid here, and certainly Napoleon III had no wish to antagonize St. Petersburg. Even more difficult was the Italian attitude. The Habsburg diplomats quite correctly insisted that an agreement should be made with Italy so that the monarchy would not have to fight on two fronts. The Italians would join in an Austro-French combination only if Napoleon III agreed to remove his troops from Rome and allow that city to become the Italian capital. Catholic French public opinion, which reacted strongly on the Roman question, tied the French emperor's hands.

Negotiations nevertheless continued. In October 1867 Francis Joseph visited Paris; military staff talks commenced in 1870, but no precise agreement was reached. At no time did the Habsburg Empire agree to go to the aid of France. In fact, it soon became obvious that if war broke out between France and Prussia the Habsburg government would wait to see who won the first battles. In contrast to the failure of France and the Habsburg Empire to come to terms, Bismarck did obtain a diplomatic victory. By April 1868 he had the assurance that if war broke out between Paris and Berlin the Russian government would act to discourage the Habsburg Empire from intervening.

Austria-Hungary was not directly involved in the question of the Hohenzollern candidacy for the Spanish throne, which led to the eventual outbreak of the Franco-Prussian War. Once hostilities commenced in July 1870, Francis Joseph met with his advisers to decide what measures should be taken. Again there was disagreement within the government. Andrassy argued strongly for neutrality, and it was this attitude that Francis Joseph finally adopted. The Habsburg decision was greatly influenced by the warnings that now came from St. Petersburg and by the presence of Russian troops on the Galician border. Because France declared war and the south German states stood with Prussia, the struggle had a German national character, which made the Prussian position popular in Austria.

The swiftness of the Prussian victories paralyzed the action of all of the powers. Both Britain and Russia had judged Prussia the weaker in this contest too. Britain was concerned chiefly about the fate of Belgium. Russia used the crisis to obtain a major foreign policy goal of her own. In October 1870 the Russian government unilaterally denounced the Black Sea clauses of the Treaty of Paris. No power was in a position to oppose this move; a congress held later accepted the Russian action.

In January 1871 the German Empire was proclaimed at Versailles. The south German states were now joined to the North German Confederation. In addition, in the peace with France the two provinces of Alsace and Lorraine were annexed by Germany. Prussia had thus in the past years demonstrated the great preponderance of her military power over both France and Austria. In this situation the Habsburg statesmen abandoned all hopes of undoing the new political arrangement in central Europe. Unified Germany was an accomplished fact. Instead, a policy of alignment and close cooperation with Berlin was to be adopted. Beust himself led in this change of policy. In 1871 he met with Bismarck at Gastein. There a long conversation took place concerning the relations of the two states. Francis Joseph and William I met at the same time in Salzburg. Although no formal agreement was signed at this time, the two powers from now on were to remain united in foreign policy.

The two events, the Ausgleich and the unification of Germany, that occurred in the short period from 1867 to 1871 were together to change the course of Habsburg history. Of the two the formation of the united Germany is perhaps the more significant from the long view of Habsburg development. With this action the empire lost its support in the German lands, and with it the German claim to leadership within the empire received a mortal blow. The German position had hitherto rested not only on the historical development of the area, but on the fact that the Austrian predominating position in the Holy Roman Empire and the Germanic Confederation had given the Germans a power base for their dominance in the monarchy. The entire state had also previously been oriented toward central Europe and toward the West. If the *grossdeutsch* solution to the German problem had been adopted, this condition could have continued. Whether all of the lands of the monarchy had or had not been included in a united Germany, the former national balance would have been maintained. Thus Bismarck, while forwarding German national interests in the Prussian sense, in fact made the major contribution to the defeat of German leadership in the Habsburg Empire.

The attempt to meet the national problem through agreement with one of the nationalities similarly weakened the ties to the empire of the others, although it is difficult to see what other alternatives were available in 1867. From a purely practical standpoint it would have been almost impossible to have established a federal solution at this time in which *all* of the nationalities would have received an equal share in the direction of the state. The strong reaction of the other peoples of the empire to the dualistic solution could, however, also be expected. The national principle had triumphed throughout central and eastern Europe. As the Slavic and Rumanian populations of the empire became increasingly aware of their own national individuality, they could not be expected to accept willingly a secondary position in a German-Magyar political organization. The entire

national question within the monarchy was also infinitely complicated by the concurrent struggle against aristocratic predominance
in Habsburg life and politics and by the interweaving of the national,
social and political revolutionary movements of the time.

By 1871 not only had the internal organization of the Habsburg
Empire changed radically, the position of the monarchy in Europe
had similarly been altered. Austria-Hungary was now surrounded
by four national states—Rumania, Serbia, Italy and Germany. Three
of these, Rumania, Serbia and Italy, still had claims on Habsburg
lands; the fourth, in contrast, needed Habsburg support. France, the
former active and aggressive power on the continent, had suffered a
severe blow to her national prestige. Napoleon III was ousted, and
by slow stages the Third Republic came into existence. French
foreign policy, once adventurous and wide in scope in its continental
involvements, now concentrated on the Rhine and on the policy of
revanche. Allied closely with Berlin, the Habsburg Monarchy in the
future was to find itself increasingly at odds with Paris, although
the two countries had few interests directly in conflict.

As has been shown above, the Habsburg Empire since 1815 had
given priority to its commitments in Italy and Germany; it had
hoped to keep its eastern frontier quiet by agreement with Russia
and by the preservation of the Ottoman Empire. In 1870, excluded
from the German and Italian lands, the empire could move forward
only in the Balkans. From 1870 to 1914 Habsburg foreign policy
was thus primarily concerned with this area; the issues of the
Eastern Question and relations with Russia became the predominant
themes of Habsburg diplomacy. The new path—alliance with Germany and a renewed interest in eastern Europe—was shown in the
diplomacy of Andrassy, who in November 1871 replaced Beust as
foreign minister.

Part III

From the Ausgleich to World War I: 1870–1914

Chapter 1

German Alliance and Balkan Revolution

The Ministry of Andrassy The Habsburg acceptance of the new central European order was indicated in the appointment of Count Julius Andrassy, the first Magyar to hold the post of foreign minister. His policies usually reflected Magyar interests in Europe, although in certain instances, particularly in 1877 and 1878, he acted against the wishes of most of his countrymen. The choice of Andrassy demonstrated the changes that had taken place within the Habsburg government since 1848 and in its attitude toward Hungary. Andrassy had been an active participant in the revolution of 1848 and a partisan of Kossuth. He had been in the Ottoman capital at the time of the defeat of the Hungarian forces and from there had made his way to western Europe. In 1857 he had been pardoned and had returned to Budapest. Abandoning the more extreme outlook of his revolutionary days, he came to stand for a policy of wide autonomy for the Hungarian lands, but not for independence. He played a large role, as has been seen, in the formulation of the Ausgleich and in the determining of Habsburg foreign policy after the 1866 disaster. He was the first prime minister of Hungary after 1867.

As foreign minister Andrassy pursued the policies he had previously advocated. He, like the Magyars of his day, saw Russia as the chief danger to the empire. He believed that the best policy for his state was that of alliance first with Germany and then with Britain and Italy. He would have liked to have formed a front of Germany, Austria-Hungary, Britain and Italy against Russia. He was a strong supporter of the maintenance of the territorial integrity of the Ottoman Empire and the political status quo in the Balkan peninsula. He did, however, favor a limited Austrian economic expansion southward. He thus approved the development of communications in the Balkans, particularly the building of railroads, but he was against the acquisition of new territory. He certainly did not wish to inaugurate a great imperial drive to the Aegean.

Andrassy's policy was thus limited in aim. While Beust before him had wished to reestablish the Habsburg position in western and central Europe, Andrassy's stand took into full account the need to recognize the changed international conditions and the fact that the empire required a period of calm to readjust to the new internal organization. The country was obviously not capable in this period of carrying on an active and aggressive foreign policy. Habsburg military weakness had been amply demonstrated in 1859 and 1866. The Ausgleich, which was to inaugurate an era of almost continual Austrian-Magyar friction over army matters, did not increase the Habsburg military potential or raise the prestige of its arms in the eyes of Europe. Habsburg policy could not be independent or daring.

Moreover, after 1870 the European diplomatic scene was dominated by Germany. Leadership in central Europe had passed decisively from Vienna to Berlin. In the same manner that Metternich had once controlled the course of events in this area the German chancellor now assumed the directing role. His chief aim was the protection of the German Empire, which had been so much his own creation. Recognizing that the French would not willingly accept the verdict of 1870, he saw his principal danger as coming from the west. In international relations he therefore sought to form an alliance system that would secure the isolation of France. Moreover, like Austria-Hungary, Germany needed a period of peace to settle the problems of internal political life arising from the unification.

As has been shown, Bismarck always completely understood the importance for Prussia of close ties with Russia. He recognized too the necessity of friendship with the Habsburg Monarchy. He had restrained William I from imposing a victor's peace in 1866. After-

ward he had immediately sought to reestablish good relations with
Vienna, but it was not until after 1870 that Beust had accepted these
views. With Andrassy in office Bismarck's endeavors were made
easier. The German chancellor was now able not only to establish
close ties with Vienna but, in addition, to effect at least a surface
reconciliation between the monarchy and Russia. Thus by 1873 the
old Holy Alliance had been resurrected in the form of the Three
Emperors' Alliance. Again the basis for the alignment was the support of the three governments for conservative political principles
and their mutual interest in the military and strategic aid they could
offer one another. All three states were also faced with internal
political conditions that made a period of tranquility in international
relations mandatory.

The first Three Emperors' Alliance did not rest primarily on any
written agreement. Its basis, like that of the Holy Alliance, was the
obvious cooperation of the three courts in international affairs and the
close relations of the rulers. It was distinctly an alignment of emperors. The friendship of the monarchs was shown in the elaborate state
visits arranged among them. In September 1872 Francis Joseph came
to Berlin. His appearance was extremely important because it signified his recognition of the new Germany. Alexander II, who
virtually invited himself, also visited the German capital at this time.
The three rulers discussed common problems, but no definite commitments were assumed. In May 1873 William I, together with Bismarck and the chief of the German general staff, Moltke, traveled to
St. Petersburg. Here a military convention was concluded in which it
was agreed that if either state were attacked by another European
power the other signatory would come to the aid of his ally. This
agreement, signed by the two emperors, never played an important
part in international affairs. In June 1873 Alexander II was invited to
Vienna, thus signifying the end of the tense relations that had
existed between the Habsburg government and Russia since the
Crimean War. Francis Joseph and Andrassy opposed adhesion to the
military convention, but a consultative agreement, the Convention of
Schönbrunn, was negotiated. In October William I visited Vienna,
and Germany adhered to this agreement. Its obligations were limited
to the stipulation that the three rulers would consult with one
another should a threat to the peace arise.

The Three Emperors' Alliance was thus a very loose arrangement
indeed. A strain was put upon it during the war scare of 1875. At

this time the French and German press carried on a heated discussion of the possibilities of a preventative war by Germany against France. Certain indications existed that perhaps Bismarck intended to carry through such an action. The situation was exploited very ably by the French foreign minister, Decazes, and both the Russian and the British governments warned Berlin. Bismarck was furious, particularly at the actions of Gorchakov, the Russian foreign minister, and his ostentatious intervention in the affair. This episode had, however, few lasting effects, and the existence of the alliance between the three courts was soon to prove of great use when the Eastern Question again came to dominate European diplomacy.

With the establishment of united Germany and Italy, the map of central and western Europe by 1870 received a settled form. No great unresolved international problems existed in this area. Certainly France would seek a reversal of the decision of 1870 and a change in her frontiers, but German military superiority and French domestic strife made it obvious that these questions would not be faced immediately. The one area in Europe that still remained in a dangerous condition of unrest was the Balkan peninsula. The triumph of the national principle in Italy, Germany and Hungary naturally had its repercussions in the east. As has been mentioned, Andrassy's basic desires here were those conforming to Magyar interests. Magyar opinion until World War I remained pro-Turkish and anti-Slav—in particular, anti-Russian. It wished to see the preservation of the Ottoman Empire because this measure best served to maintain the balance of power in eastern Europe. The Magyars also felt a certain kinship with the Turks through their common Uralic-Altaic language.

Indeed, from the Habsburg point of view the alternatives to the maintenance of the empire all seemed bad. There were three possible solutions: first, that Russia would replace the Ottoman Empire as the power in control of the Balkan peninsula; second, that Austria-Hungary and Russia would divide the area into equal spheres of influence; and third, that the Balkan states would share the territory among themselves. Serbia, Montenegro, Greece and Rumania were already autonomous or independent political units. They all wished to enlarge their lands. A Bulgarian and an Albanian state could also be formed. Of these possibilities, quite obviously the first alternative, Russian domination, would present a real menace to the Habsburg Empire. It would also have been strongly opposed by Britain. The second, a partition, was similarly disliked because it would probably lead to Habsburg acquisition of more territory inhabited by South Slavs. The Magyar leaders consistently attempted to block the addition of more Slavic people to the empire. Moreover, the lands that could be acquired were impoverished and backward. The finances of the empire were already in a poor condition. Added military, administrative and other expenses could not be borne with ease. The third alternative, the division of the Balkans into national states, also presented great dangers. Most feared was the construction of a large Slavic state that would have the territory and resources sufficient to control the Balkans. As will be seen, Austria-Hungary first opposed a great Bulgaria, and then a great Serbia. Of these two states the Habsburg government was more apprehensive about a growth in Serbian strength because of the relations of the Serbs with the South Slavs of the empire.

However, despite these drawbacks certain groups within the monarchy were willing to accept the second alternative and to participate in a partition of the Ottoman Empire. Habsburg interests were most directly involved in the adjacent provinces of Bosnia and Hercegovina. Because of the position of these lands in relation to Dalmatia, some military leaders advised that they should be annexed as a protection to the Habsburg Adriatic possessions. Moreover, Francis Joseph always thought in dynastic terms. He had recently been compelled to give Lombardy and Venetia to Italy; the acquisition of Bosnia and Hercegovina would balance this loss. He, like Alexander II, viewed the surrender of land as a personal matter and a stain on his honor and that of his house.

In Balkan affairs, as has been seen, Austria-Hungary had chiefly to deal with Russia. Germany's interests lay predominantly in securing agreement between her two allies so that the Three Emperors' Alliance would not be endangered. Despite the fact that in the first half of the century the Russian government had usually wished to maintain the Ottoman Empire, after the Crimean War its policy shifted more to the support of the creation of autonomous Balkan states. Because of the defeat in 1856 and the great reforms of the 1860s, Russia did not follow an active policy in the Near East for over a decade. Internal reorganization and the breaking of the clauses of the Treaty of Paris referring to the neutralization of the

Black Sea had to be accomplished first. In 1870 Russia had denounced these provisions, and thereafter her interest in Balkan affairs increased.

Relations between Russia and the Habsburg Empire were to be
complicated by the rise of Panslavism in Russia after the Crimean
War. This movement was the Russian equivalent of the intense national feelings that were present throughout Europe and was a natural reaction to the humiliation of the defeat in the Crimean War.
As has been shown, there was always a great deal of deep sympathy
in Russia for the fate of the Slavic Orthodox Christians under
Moslem rule. Before the Crimean War the Slavophiles had emphasized the unique and superior qualities of the Slavic peoples.
After 1856 these currents came together in the various Panslav programs. Although the political aims of those who espoused the Panslav cause differed widely, all called for Russian leadership in the
Slavic world, the liberation of the Slavs under foreign control and
their formation into some sort of organization in which Russia
would play the predominant role. The implications of these ideas
for the Balkans and for the Habsburg Empire were clear. Previously
Russian policy in the Balkans had been based on religion, that is,
on assisting Christians under Moslem rule. The Panslavs wished to
shift the emphasis from the religious to the national basis. Their
program was obviously directed primarily against the Ottoman Empire, but it could be applied against the Habsburg Empire, which
also held control of Slavic peoples. As the Ottoman Empire during
the second half of the nineteenth century was gradually pushed from
Europe, the significance of Austria-Hungary, as the major power with
a large Slavic population held in a position of political subordination,
grew. The enemy of the Panslavs then became not the "Turk" but
the "German." It should be strongly emphasized that Panslavism was
more effective as a cultural than as a political program and that it was
not endorsed by the Russian government. Until her own collapse in
1917 tsarist Russia never contemplated the destruction of the Habsburg Empire. The continued existence of this state was always regarded as essential for the balance of power in Europe and the
protection of conservative political principles.

The center of the Panslav movement in Russia was Moscow, not
St. Petersburg. Here the Slavic Benevolent Society, formed in 1858,
was the center for wide educational and political activities. Branches
of this organization were established in other cities. Many were

attracted to the movement not because of its specific doctrines but because it affirmed the superiority of the Slavs, the Russians in particular, in a time of internal difficulties and when the German people seemed to be in the process of swift ascendency. Although "official" Russia stood against the Panslavs, the program attracted the support of many influential members of the government. Most important was the interest shown in the movement by the heir to the throne, the future Alexander III, and the practical assistance offered by the ambassador in Constantinople, N. P. Ignatiev. Panslav ideas were also propagated by extremely able writers and publicists, in particular, I. S. Aksakov and M. N. Katkov.

Soon after its founding, the Slavic Benevolent Society began to concern itself actively with Balkan conditions. It established scholarships for students, and many Bulgarians, in particular, studied at Russian educational institutions. In 1867 an exhibition was held in Moscow, and another in 1868 in Prague. These organizations and their publications attracted wide attention in Europe, where they were accredited with an influence on Russian policy that they did not in fact possess. This active and vocal group, which called for the reassertion of a strong Russian role in international relations, did, however, play a major part in pushing Russia into another Balkan conflict.

Like Russia and Austria-Hungary, Britain remained at this time intensely concerned over the fate of the Ottoman Empire. During this century British and French investments and economic involvement in the Near East had been greatly increased. The Turkish railroads and other enterprises rested on western European capital. In 1869 the Suez Canal was opened. Thereafter the eastern Mediterranean became the main route for all the nations to the Far East. Since the canal was within Ottoman territory, its fate, and that of Egypt, became of even more interest to the Western powers.

A new Eastern crisis was commenced in 1875 by a revolt of the peasants of Hercegovina against their landlords. The insurrection was caused chiefly by local agrarian conditions and was directed against a class that was South Slav in nationality although Moslem in religion. The movement had immediate repercussions in both Russia and Austria-Hungary. Thousands of refugees crossed into the monarchy, where they had to be fed and housed. In Russia a great deal of sympathy was felt for the plight of the Christian rebels. When the Ottoman government was unable to restore order in the area, the great powers found themselves again forced to intervene in Balkan affairs. In 1875 and 1876 the three conservative courts sponsored reform programs that they hoped would calm the revolt. These were submitted to the Ottoman Empire and the other powers. Another effort at obtaining a settlement was the Andrassy Note of December 1875, which was drawn up by the Habsburg minister and the Russian ambassador in Vienna. When this proposal was rejected by the rebels a further attempt to calm the situation was made. In May 1876 Gorchakov, Bismarck and Andrassy met and formulated the Berlin Memorandum. Britain, now under the leadership of Disraeli, refused to adhere to this plan, an action that encouraged the Ottoman Empire to follow her example.

Meanwhile, during the negotiations, the revolt spread. In April 1876 the Bulgarians too rose in rebellion. The atrocities committed by the Turks in suppressing the uprising received wide attention in Europe. In addition, at the same time the Russian government was carrying on discussions with the powers to try to find a peaceful solution to the crisis, the Slavic committees in Russia were organizing aid for the rebels. After the outbreak of the revolt in Bosnia and Hercegovina the neighboring Slavic states of Serbia and Montenegro had soon become involved. The Slavic committees now sent large quantities of military and medical supplies to these people, and Russian volunteers streamed into Serbia. In June and July Serbia and Montenegro went to war against the Ottoman Empire; their armies were led by the Russian General M. G. Cherniaev. Despite their enthusiasm for the cause, the Balkan states were almost immediately defeated. In October the Russian government was forced to intervene and deliver an ultimatum to Constantinople to prevent the complete destruction of the two Balkan armies.

Although the Turkish military forces were thus victorious, conditions in the Ottoman capital had been anything but stable. In May Sultan Abdul Aziz was deposed. His successor, Murad V, was himself replaced in August by Abdul Hamid II. Chaos in the central government and the national ferment in the South Slav lands under Ottoman rule placed the great powers in a difficult position. Once again it appeared that the Ottoman Empire might simply collapse. Undoubtedly the strongest pressure to act was exerted upon Alexander II. Although both the tsar and his chief advisers preferred a policy of cooperation with the powers, it was apparent that this method of dealing with the Balkan crisis was not leading to any favorable results. Even Andrassy, who had consistently supported the maintenance of the empire, now had to face the possibility that another solution might have to be found.

Throughout the events of this period Bismarck was chiefly concerned lest his two allies clash. He favored the cooperation of Austria-Hungary and Russia and their agreement on the partition of the Balkans into spheres of influence. He had little sympathy with either the maintenance of the territorial integrity of the Ottoman Empire or the rights of the Balkan nationalities. The concept of partition also could be of advantage to the Russian government. Since it now seemed that war with the Ottoman Empire was inevitable, Russia had to be sure of the position of the Habsburg Empire. She could not risk a repeat of the condition that had arisen in the Crimean War. In July 1876 Andrassy and Gorchakov met at Reichstadt to discuss the general Balkan situation. Since no written agreement was made, there was later to be great disagreement over the details of the conversations. At this time Serbia and Montenegro were at war with the Ottoman Empire, so provision had to be made for a possible settlement of this conflict. It was therefore agreed that if the Turks were victorious, Austria-Hungary and Russia would insist that the status quo ante be restored and that reforms be introduced in Bosnia and Hercegovina. In other words, even if it won, the Ottoman government would not be allowed to profit from the victory. If the Turkish armies were defeated, however, the two powers agreed to the partition of the empire. A Bulgarian and a Rumelian state were to be formed; Greece was to receive Epirus and Thessaly. Constantinople might become a free city. Russia was to take territorial compensation with the acquisition of Batum and the southern Bessarabian districts, which had been lost in 1856. There was later disagreement on what was awarded Austria-Hungary, but she was given part, if not all, of Bosnia and Hercegovina. In this agreement the Habsburg government reversed its former policy of the conservation of the empire and instead joined with Russia in a program for its destruction.

Even with this understanding the Russian government did not feel sure of what the Habsburg attitude would be in a time of real crisis. Andrassy had consistently refused to take part in any military action against the Porte. It was thus essential that Russia make certain of the German position. Inquiries were next made in Berlin to discover what Germany would do should Russia and Austria-Hungary become involved in a war over Balkan issues. This was a question Bismarck did not wish to answer. Pressed by the Russian government, he finally replied that Germany would remain neutral, but that she could not afford to see the Habsburg Empire so decisively defeated that it no longer held the rank of a great power. This answer greatly disturbed the Russian statesmen. They felt they were not being repaid for their benevolent attitude during the Prussian unification of Germany. The German reply, however, moderated Russian action and showed St. Petersburg that full agreement with Vienna was absolutely necessary before a war could be embarked upon.

Like the Crimean War, the Russo-Turkish War of 1877 took a long time to start. The powers continued to negotiate to try to find a solution. In December 1876 a conference was held in Constantinople and more reform proposals were offered, but the problem of securing Turkish acceptance remained. On December 23 the Turkish government announced a new constitution, which, it argued, made the reforms sponsored by the European powers unnecessary. After the failure of the Constantinople Conference the Russian government continued to negotiate, but preparations for war were accelerated. Since agreement could not be reached with the powers, the Russians now made very sure of Habsburg support. In January and March, 1877, agreements were signed in which Austria-Hungary promised to maintain an attitude of benevolent neutrality in a war between Russia and the Ottoman Empire. In return, she was to acquire Bosnia and Hercegovina; the fate of the Sanjak of Novi Bazar, a small strip of territory separating Serbia and Montenegro, was to be decided later. Russia was to take southern Bessarabia. No provision was made for Russian acquisitions in Asia Minor or for the establishment of a Bulgarian state, but it was stipulated that no large Balkan state should be set up. Russia also agreed that Serbia and Montenegro should not be a zone of combat. Russian armies were to operate strictly outside of these lands.

The Habsburg government thus again accepted the partition of European Turkey. According to these agreements a Russian victory in the war would bring about the solution to the Balkan problem that Bismarck wanted—the establishment of Russian predominance in the eastern half of the Balkan peninsula, Habsburg control in the western part. Provision had been made against the construction of a state large enough to dominate the area and to threaten the Habsburg Empire. The assurance appeared to have been gained that a Russo-Turkish war, followed by the collapse of Ottoman power in the peninsula, would not mean Russian domination of the Balkans. Austria-Hungary was, in addition, to acquire two provinces without a war.

With these arrangements made, the Russian government could now with greater safety launch a war. An agreement on passage was made with Rumania, and on April 24, 1877, hostilities were commenced. Contrary to Russian expectations, the war proved very difficult to win. At first the Russians had been very confident. They refused Serbian and Rumanian aid because they did not think it would be needed, and they preferred to remain unencumbered by allies. After major defeats at Plevna in July and September, they were forced to request assistance from the other Balkan nations. Throughout the war the Habsburg government remained loyal to its agreements with Russia. Both the Habsburg and the British governments had a similar interest in preventing the establishment of stronger Russian influence in the Balkans. They exchanged notes, but their relations continued to be marred by the feeling of mutual distrust so often apparent in previous years.

The great difficulties encountered in the campaign and the high losses sustained resulted in the increase of influence in the Russian government and army of those who wished to make a victor's peace and to negotiate a settlement with the Ottoman Empire without the participation of the other European powers. In December Alexander II approved a program for peace that was in strong contradiction with the terms of his previous accords with Austria-Hungary and that would have upset the balance of power in the Balkans. Most significant for the Habsburg government was the proposal to create a large Bulgarian state and to have it occupied for two years by Russian armies. No mention was made of Habsburg control of Bosnia-Hercegovina. When these conditions were transmitted to Russia's ally, the reaction of Vienna could be expected. Francis Joseph immediately protested against these two stipulations, which most directly involved his interests. Despite the strong disapproval of the Russian actions, the Russian government did not abandon its plans. After the fall of Plevna in December, the Russian armies advanced quickly toward Constantinople. In January 1878 the Ottoman government appealed for a cessation of hostilities. At the end of January, with its armies on the outskirts of the Turkish capital,

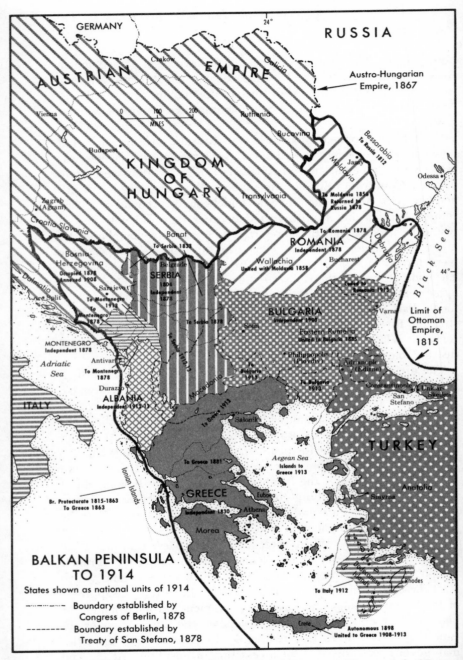

GERMANY

RUSSIA

AUSTRIAN EMPIRE

Crakow

Galicia

24°

Austro-Hungarian
Empire, 1867

Vienna

Ruthenia

Bucovina

Bessarabia
To Russia 1812

Budapest

KINGDOM
OF
HUNGARY

Moldavia

Jassy

Odessa

Transylvania

To Moldavia 1856
Returned to
Russia 1878

44°

Zagreb
(Agram)

Croatia-Slavonia

Banat
To Serbia 1833

ROMANIA
Independent 1878

Dobrudja

To Romania 1878

Dalmatia

Bosnia-
Herzegovina
Occupied 1878
Annexed 1908

Belgrade

Wallachia
United with Moldavia 1858

Bucharest

Black Sea

Fiume
Split

Sarajevo

SERBIA
1804
Independent
1878

Ceded to
Romania 1913

To Serbia 1878

MONTENEGRO
Independent 1878

To Montenegro
1913

To Montenegro
1878

To Serbia 1912-13

BULGARIA
Independent 1908

Sofia

Eastern Rumelia
United to Bulgaria 1885

Varna

Limit of
Ottoman
Empire,
1815

Adriatic
Sea

Antivar
To Montenegro
1878

Durazzo

ALBANIA
Independent 1912-13

Macedonia

Philippopolis
(Plovdiv)

To
Bulgaria
1913

Adrianople
(Edirne)

To Bulgaria
1913

Constantinople

Unkiar
Skelessi

ITALY

To Greece 1913

Salonika

San
Stefano

TURKEY

Ionian Islands

To Greece 1881

Aegean Sea

Islands to
Greece 1913

Anatolia

Smyrna

Br. Protectorate 1815-1863
To Greece 1863

GREECE
Independent 1830

Euboea

Athens

Morea

To Italy 1912

Rhodes

BALKAN PENINSULA
TO 1914

States shown as national units of 1914

—··—··— Boundary established by
Congress of Berlin, 1878

———— Boundary established by
Treaty of San Stefano, 1878

Crete
Autonomous 1898
United to Greece 1908-1913

From Bryce Lyon, Herbert Rowen, and Theodore S. Hamerow, *A History of the Western World* (Chicago: Rand McNally & Company, 1969), p. 689. Cartography by Willis R. Heath.

the Russian government made an armistice agreement incorporating the provisions previously mentioned. A European crisis immediately followed. In the middle of February the British fleet entered the Straits; at the same time the Habsburg government considered the question of war. Despite these ominous signs the Russians concluded on March 3, the Treaty of San Stefano with the Ottoman government. This agreement provided for the creation of a large Bulgarian state, the granting of independence to Rumania and Serbia and an increase of territory to Serbia and Montenegro. Russia acquired for her part southern Bessarabia and territories in Asia Minor. Bosnia-Herce-govina was left under Ottoman administration.

These provisions met with strong Austrian and British protests. Britain was concerned chiefly with the Asiatic settlement, Austria-Hungary with the status of Bosnia and Hercegovina. Both opposed the creation of a large Bulgarian state. Faced with the combined pressure of the powers the Russian government was forced to agree to Andrassy's proposal that a congress be held to consider the terms of the Treaty of San Stefano. Russia could not risk a war on the issue. Before this meeting opened in Berlin, the main lines of the final settlement had been decided upon. In an understanding concluded with Britain in May Russia agreed to reduce the size of the Bul-garian state and to limit her gains in Asia. Britain also made an agreement with the Habsburg Empire on the Bulgarian question and the future of Bosnia.

At the Congress of Berlin, which opened on June 13 and lasted a month, Andrassy was able to secure the recognition of the powers of the right of Austria-Hungary to occupy and administer the two provinces of Bosnia and Hercegovina. This action met with great opposition from the Ottoman Empire. Only when the Habsburg government agreed to sign a special treaty with the Porte in which Turkish sovereignty was reaffirmed did the Ottoman delegates agree to the proposal. The question of Novi Pazar caused considerable friction between the Habsburg Empire and Russia. Andrassy wished to acquire this territory in order to assure that this line of separation between the two South Slav states would be retained. At the con-gress Austria-Hungary won the right to occupy the area. Andrassy also sought to restrict Serbian and Montenegrin gains as much as possible. He was particularly concerned about the awarding of a port on the Adriatic to Montenegro. Although he was not able to prevent this state from receiving Antivari, its use was restricted. In addition to these successes, Austria-Hungary obtained a settlement of the Bulgarian question in her interest. The large Bulgaria of the San Stefano treaty was divided into three sections. The first, Bulgaria proper, was made into an autonomous principality; the second, Eastern Rumelia, was returned to Turkish administration but was to be allowed a Christian governor and certain reforms. The third, Macedonia, went back to Ottoman rule.

Viewed as a whole, the settlement made at the Congress of Berlin was a Habsburg success. It represented the continuation of the policy adopted at Reichstadt, that is, of the partition of the Balkans into spheres of influence. At the congress the Russian government abandoned the Serbs and concentrated on gaining advantages for the Bulgarians. The Serbian representatives were plainly told to look to Vienna. After the conference it was generally recognized that Russia would predominate in Bulgaria while Austria-Hungary for her share would control the western half of the Balkans. The strong reaction of the Rumanian government to the loss of southern Bessarabia to Russia led it to turn in the next years to the Habsburg Empire for support. Thus in 1878 the Habsburg government enjoyed the strongest position that it had held in the Balkans in the century. It had a clear position of supremacy in the western half, and it was to be allied with Rumania. Russian influence in the eastern Balkans was limited to the small Bulgarian state.

Despite these great gains Andrassy did not receive a triumphant welcome home. Francis Joseph among others did not like the terms of the occupation of Bosnia and Hercegovina. He would have preferred a direct annexation. In contrast, the Magyar leaders were displeased with the acquisition of more Slavic peoples in the empire. Moreover, the administration of the provinces immediately posed a problem. They could not be incorporated into either Austria or Hungary without upsetting the balance within the monarchy. They were therefore placed under the control of the minister of finance of the joint government. This very unsatisfactory arrangement hampered the future administration of the area.

In addition the new rulers found that their control was anything but welcome in the provinces. The Habsburg statesmen had thought that they would march their troops into the lands with flags waving and that they would be greeted with pleasure by the inhabitants. Instead they met strong resistance, especially from the Moslems, and in the end they had to wage a regular campaign to subdue the territory. In 1881 another revolt broke out, extending also to southern Dalmatia. The protests this time were directed against Habsburg taxation and conscription. Although the rebellion was put down, the cost in men and money was high. Thereafter in their administration of the provinces the Habsburg officials made a real effort to govern well. However, as had also been the experience in Lombardy-Venetia, the local population felt extreme dissatisfaction with Habsburg rule and with the lack of institutions of local self-government. The area thus remained a center of discontent and unrest.

Despite the fact that it did achieve a peaceful settlement between the great powers, the Congress of Berlin was regarded by most Russians as a defeat, and it had a disastrous effect upon the Three Emperors' Alliance. Russia had waged a costly campaign and had been forced to submit the final settlement to the judgment of Europe. In the peace only southern Bessarabia and Batum had been annexed. The client state of Bulgaria had been drastically reduced in size. The Russian reaction was particularly strong against Germany and Bismarck personally. The Russian government had expected more support from Berlin, largely because of Russian aid to Prussia in the previous years. The Three Emperors' Alliance was thus for all practical purposes dissolved in 1878.

The loosening of the ties with St. Petersburg caused little worry in Vienna. Andrassy had never been an enthusiastic proponent of the alignment. Bismarck, however, was thoroughly alarmed. He now came to the conclusion that Germany's interests demanded the formation of a strong alliance with the Habsburg Empire. His main problem lay in convincing William I of the necessity of an understanding with Austria-Hungary apart from Russia. The German emperor still favored close relations with St. Petersburg and regarded a separate link with the Habsburg Monarchy as a betrayal of Russia. Bismarck discussed the entire question with Andrassy in August 1879. The Habsburg minister favored the proposal, and Francis Joseph also approved. Andrassy, however, differed with Bismarck on the terms of the alliance. Concerned chiefly with Germany's relations with France, Bismarck wished to conclude a general defensive pact. Andrassy, looking eastward, wanted an agreement that would be directed exclusively against Russia. Not only did the German chancellor meet with resistance from his own ruler, but

Andrassy continued to insist on his point of view. Finally, under intense pressure from Bismarck, the German crown prince Frederick and most of his advisers, William I accepted not only a treaty but one that was directed against St. Petersburg.

The Dual Alliance of 1879 was certainly the most important single document signed by the Habsburg government in the period under discussion in this survey. The alliance was purely defensive; in the treaty both Germany and Austria-Hungary agreed to assist each other should Russia attack either partner. If either state were involved in a war with another power, the other signatory would remain neutral unless Russia entered. The agreement was for five years and was to be kept secret. It was renewed periodically and was in effect at the outbreak of World War I. The advantages to Austria-Hungary were obvious. Germany was now obligated to come to the aid of the monarchy in the event of a Russian attack. No similar obligation was assumed by the empire in case of a French move against Germany. Austria-Hungary thus had some assurance that Germany would back her Balkan position in case of a repetition of the events of the 1870s. The alliance also brought central Europe back to much the same diplomatic condition in which it had been before the unification of Germany, but the leadership now lay in the hands of Berlin. In 1848 the *kleindeutsch* solution for the German problem had been the union of the German lands without the monarchy, but the joining of the united nation with Vienna in a tight alliance. The Dual Alliance had achieved this combination.

For both partners, of course, the pact had disadvantages as well as advantages. Although Vienna now gained support against Russia, the agreement involved the monarchy in Germany's quarrels with France. When after 1890 Germany and Britain also came increasingly into conflict, Austria-Hungary found herself estranged from another power with whom she had no real disagreements. In return, Germany was drawn into Balkan entanglements that did not affect her interests directly. The conclusion of the pact was, in addition, to inaugurate a new development in international relations that was to prove dangerous to the peace and stability of Europe in the future. From 1815 to 1879 there had been few formal alliances in existence. The British government had steadfastly refused to. sign such pacts. The Holy Alliance and the Three Emperors' Alliance had been based upon the common bonds between the monarchs rather than on the agreements made between them. After 1879 the powers of Europe came to base their security more often on regular treaties. The grouping of the powers and their formation into rival camps were to contribute greatly to the change in atmosphere in international relations after the turn of the century.

Following the completion of the alliance, Andrassy resigned his office. Although he had not been uniformly successful, his career as Hungarian prime minister and Habsburg foreign minister had been eventful. He had played a major part in the formation of the Ausgleich, he had led his country through the dangers of the Balkan crisis of 1875–1878, and he had acquired control of Bosnia and Hercegovina. Finally, he had brought Austria-Hungary back into close association with Germany. Although these acts led in the future to grave complications, Andrassy's accomplishments at the time of his retirement appeared indeed noteworthy.

The Ministry of Haymerle   As his successor Andrassy would have preferred the Habsburg representative in Berlin, Count Gustav Kalnoky, but upon his refusal Heinrich von Haymerle became foreign minister for the relatively brief period between October 1879 and October 1881. Born into a German family, Haymerle had been ambassador in Italy. During his term in office he proved to be a hesitant and careful diplomat. His chief concern was to preserve and protect the position won for the empire by Andrassy in European affairs. He was involved in the controversies over the Greek and Montenegrin borders, arising from the implementation of the decisions of the Congress of Berlin, but his chief activity was concerned with the continuation of the alliance network that had commenced with the Dual Alliance.

At the Congress of Berlin, as has been mentioned, Austria-Hungary gained a position of practical predominance in the affairs of Serbia. With Habsburg assistance the Serbs had acquired possession of Pirot and Niš. With its new position in Bosnia-Hercegovina, it became even more important for the Habsburg government to maintain a close relationship with Belgrade. Vienna thus next attempted to obtain formal political commitments from the Serbian government. The Serbian ruler, Milan Obrenović, proved a willing collaborator. After having been rejected by Russia, he had no alternative but to comply with the Habsburg desires. In May 1881 a commercial treaty beneficial to the monarchy was signed. Most important, however, was the alliance of June 1881. Here the Serbian government agreed to suppress any conspiracies directed against the Habsburg government and not to make any agreements with other states that were contrary to the spirit of this treaty. In a secret letter Milan strengthened this second provision by promising to conclude no treaties that were not previously approved by Austria-Hungary. These conditions made Serbia a satellite of the monarchy. Austria-Hungary thus obtained in Belgrade much the same position that Russia at the time enjoyed in Sofia. The weakness in the relationship was the basic hostility of the Serbs to a pro-Habsburg orientation. Milan was forced to keep the agreement strictly secret because he knew that his people would not approve it. The treaty was renewed in 1889 to extend for six more years.

In return for his compliant attitude, Milan received from the Habsburg government support for his dynasty. In 1882 he was able to take the title of king. He also obtained some vague promises of Habsburg assistance for future Serbian acquisitions in Macedonia. After the division of the large Bulgaria of San Stefano, Bulgaria, Serbia and Greece all looked upon Macedonia as the next field for their own national expansion; all sought great-power backing for their claims. The Serbian government now felt that it had the support of Austria-Hungary for its policy in the south.

The main accomplishment of Haymerle's ministry was the renewal of the Three Emperors' Alliance, which had been broken at the Congress of Berlin. The impulsion for this move came from Berlin and St. Petersburg, not from Vienna. Bismarck always wished to maintain German relations with Russia since his main concern was with France; Russia needed an alliance because she feared a position of diplomatic isolation. Since Germany was associated with the Habsburg Empire in the Dual Alliance, Bismarck preferred that the monarchy also be a partner in any revived German-Russian alignment. The Habsburg government did not receive the idea with enthusiasm. Russia remained the chief threat to Habsburg interests in the Balkans. Austria-Hungary had the security it needed in the Dual Alliance; no clear advantage could be gained from an extension of Habsburg commitments. If further alliances were to be made, the Habsburg government wished that they be made with Britain, who could aid in blocking Russian advances in the Near East. Hopes for a tie with London, however, faded when Gladstone and the Liberal party came to power in 1880. Before the election the British states-man made his famous pronouncement on the Habsburg Empire. Austria, he declared, had been

> the unflinching foe of freedom in every country in Europe.... There is not an instance—there is not a spot upon the whole map where you can lay your finger and say: "There Austria did good."[13]

Although Gladstone later apologized for this remark, Austria-Hungary continued to find little support in Britain as long as the Liberal party was in control. Bismarck also exerted strong pressure in Vienna to influence the government to agree to a new treaty with Russia. Under these circumstances Haymerle gradually came to accept the German arguments.

In March 1881 Alexander II was assassinated. The new tsar, Alexander III, had been known as strongly nationalistic and as a supporter of Panslav programs during the previous Eastern crisis. Nevertheless, on his accession he made it clear that he would continue his father's policy of seeking a closer association with Berlin and Vienna. The Three Emperors' Alliance thus again came into existence, this time in the form of a written agreement in which the obligations of the partners were defined. In the treaty of June 1881 the three powers agreed that if one of their number were engaged in a war, even of an offensive nature, with another great power, the others would remain neutral. The signatories also promised to consult one another on any changes in the status quo in the Ottoman Empire. Russia gained from her allies the recognition of her position on the Straits question and their assent to unite Eastern Rumelia and Bulgaria should the opportunity arise. Austria-Hungary was conceded the right to annex Bosnia-Hercegovina in the future. Germany for her part received the assurance that if she went to war with France, Russia would remain neutral.

The Ministry of Kalnoky   The policies of Andrassy and of Haymerle, who died in office, were continued by the next foreign minister, Gustav Kalnoky. Like his predecessors he was conservative in disposition, and he had no desire to advance upon adventurous policies.

---

[13] Seton-Watson, *Britain in Europe*, p. 549.

He too favored the continuation of close ties with Berlin. The fact that previously he had been ambassador in St. Petersburg emphasized the Habsburg desire to maintain a policy of cooperation with Russia. During the first period of his ministry he completed the formation of the alliance system initiated by Andrassy with the conclusion of treaties with Italy and Rumania. During this time, as in the previous period, Germany continued to exert great influence upon Habsburg policy. The Habsburg diplomats were still to be drawn into diplomatic combinations favored primarily by Bismarck.

In the years after 1870 Italy had played a remarkably quiet role in international relations. The government was absorbed with the problems attendant on the unification. The question of the Papacy, involving relations with France, and the issue of the *irredenta,* affecting its ties with Austria-Hungary, continued to cause irritation between the new state and its neighbors. Moreover, the Italian government had to decide the future direction of its foreign affairs. It could either concentrate on a continental policy and attempt to gain Trieste and the south Tyrol, which would involve hostility toward Vienna, or it could try to create a Mediterranean empire on the model of ancient Rome, which would bring the state into conflict with France.

The weakness of the Italian position in international affairs was shown clearly at the Congress of Berlin. The Italian representative, Count Corti, had not pressed any particular claims on the part of Italy, but when he came home with empty hands the outcry was loud. Britain had picked up Cyprus, and Austria-Hungary had acquired Bosnia and Hercegovina. An even worse blow to Italian ambitions occurred in 1881. At this time, with British and German encouragement, France took Tunis, a territory upon which Italian eyes had also been cast. It was now obvious that Italy needed allies if a policy of expansion was to be adopted. Even before the Congress of Berlin the Italian government had approached Germany, but Bismarck then saw no advantage in an Italian alliance. After the French conquest of Tunis, when the Italian government regarded France as its principal opponent, the possible basis for an agreement became clearer. Bismarck was always willing to join an anti-French combination. At the time neither Berlin nor Vienna held a high opinion of Italy's military prowess, but the country occupied an important strategic position. In alliance with Germany, Italy could force France to concentrate troops on the Alps frontier as well as on the Rhine. An agreement with Rome would assure Vienna of security on her southern front if war broke out with Russia in the east.

Although an alliance with Italy did offer some advantages, the Habsburg statesmen were hesitant when the idea was first considered. Italy also was more interested in securing Germany as an ally. Bismarck nevertheless insisted that the Habsburg government be a partner to the pact. Kalnoky at first resisted; he saw no gains for his country in an alignment directed against France. If a treaty were to be made, he preferred a simple neutrality agreement. In the end, however, he accepted Bismarck's arguments. The final document, signed in May 1882, was primarily a defensive treaty against a French attack on Italy or Germany. Its terms provided that should France attack Italy, Austria-Hungary and Germany would come to her aid. Should any of the signatories be at war with another power, the others would remain neutral. Should a third power enter, the other partners would be obligated to render assistance.

The treaty was thus of obvious use to Italy and Germany, both of whom felt immediately threatened by France. During the negotiations the Italian government had insisted that it be made clear that the agreement was not directed against Britain. It should be noted that throughout the next years the Italians remained most concerned that their relations with Britain not be endangered. British sea power in the Mediterranean gave that state a strong position in Rome. Since German relations with Britain were now good, the interests of Berlin and Rome were identical in this matter. The treaty, however, offered little to aid the third partner. It did not deal with major Habsburg problems in international relations, or even with the main points in dispute between Vienna and Rome. Although after the signature of the agreement the Italian government did not openly pursue the *irredenta* issue, these questions continued to disturb Italian public opinion. Moreover, the alliance did not strengthen the Habsburg position against Russia as it did the Italians in their relations with the French. Italy undertook no obligations to aid the empire in case of a Russian attack. The question of the Papacy also remained. After the occupation of the city of Rome by the Italian troops in 1870, the pope withdrew to the Vatican and refused to recognize the new state. Francis Joseph as a Catholic monarch was naturally affected by the conflict between the pope and the Italian government.

The agreement of 1882 was strictly continental in emphasis. Italy was promised no assistance in the colonial field. The treaty re-established the relationship throughout all of central Europe that we have seen in Metternich's time. Italy, Austria-Hungary and the German lands again formed a great diplomatic block, although now, of course, the direction lay in the hands of Bismarck and not in those of a Habsburg minister. The Triple Alliance, like the Three Emperors' Alliance, had an ideological side; the three monarchs of this alignment were also associated in a policy of common cooperation against republican elements.

After the signature of the treaty Italian-Habsburg relations did not measurably improve. In 1881 the Italian ruler came to Vienna. Much hard feeling was caused by Francis Joseph's failure to return the visit, but the Catholic monarch could not stay in Rome as long as the relations between the Italian government and the Vatican remained unsettled. The next years were also marked by an increase of irredentist agitation among the Italian public. Of particular significance was the Oberdan case. A student, Guglielmo Oberdan, was arrested in Trieste with bombs in his possession with which he had intended to assassinate Francis Joseph. He was then tried and executed. He thereafter was regarded as a martyr to the Italian cause by the intense patriots. Relations between Italy and Austria-Hungary could not be close under these conditions. Each pursued her own course in international relations; the chief tie remained Bismarck's interest in maintaining the alliance.

Like the Italian alignment, Austria-Hungary's treaty with Rumania in 1883 was reached by way of Berlin. After the Congress of Berlin the Rumanian government was bitter and fearful. Despite an agreement signed in April 1877 that it would protect Rumanian territorial integrity, the Russian government in 1878 took back from Rumania southern Bessarabia and gave her in return the less valuable northern Dobrudja. Thereafter Rumania turned to Germany to seek support against any future Russian threats to her independence or her lands. Bismarck insisted, however, that any agreement should be made first with Vienna.

In the past years Rumanian relations with the Habsburg Monarchy had not been particularly smooth. In 1875 a commercial treaty had been concluded that was very advantageous to Vienna. There had been friction subsequently over matters connected with the construction of railroads and the international administration of the Danube River. The chief hindrance to friendly relations was the problem of the approximately 2,800,000 Rumanians who lived in Austria-Hungary. The main point of contention was the status of the Rumanian population of Transylvania, which was in a position of political and cultural subservience to the dominant Magyar minority. This relationship was to deteriorate even further as the years passed with the increasing efforts of Magyarization made by the Budapest government and the parallel rise of Rumanian national self-consciousness. The question of the *irredenta* at issue between Rumania and the empire overshadowed in importance the similar conflict with Italy. Austria-Hungary could afford to give up, if absolutely necessary, the south Tyrol and perhaps Trieste, but the loss of Transylvania would be difficult to contemplate except in the case of the dissolution of the empire. In the 1880s this problem was not immediate. For the moment the Rumanian government was more concerned about the danger from Russia. Its chief fear was that its northern neighbor might reestablish the control it had held over Rumanian internal affairs before the Crimean War. In addition, the ruler of the country, Charles, was a Hohenzollern prince with strong German connections. He naturally favored a tie with the central European powers.

The agreement of 1883 between the Habsburg Empire and Rumania was a defensive treaty aimed at Russia. Its duration was five years, but it was renewed at regular intervals until 1916. Germany adhered immediately; Italy joined in 1889. The advantages for Austria-Hungary were great. Not only did she receive the promise of assistance in case of a war with Russia, but through this pact the main Russian road to Constantinople was blocked. The understanding also appeared to carry some guarantee that the Rumanian government would not pursue an active irredentist policy in regard to Transylvania.

The signature of this pact marked the completion of Bismarck's system of alliances. Although Germany was the dominant member of the alignment, Vienna was the key to the network. The monarchy was joined by major agreements with Rome, Berlin and St. Petersburg. Her Balkan position was extremely strong through the pacts with Belgrade and Bucharest. In 1884 the Three Emperors' Alliance was renewed for three years. If treaties could guarantee Habsburg security, a virtually ideal situation had been created. A major crisis in Bulgaria in 1885 was to disturb the tranquility of Europe and to test the utility of these alliances as instruments in international relations.

The chief advantage Russia had gained at the Congress of Berlin had been the recognition by the powers of the autonomous Bulgarian state and the special position St. Petersburg would enjoy there. The Russian government had supervised the establishment of the Bulgarian administration and had suggested the name of the prince, Alexander of Battenberg, who was to be the ruler of the new state. Russia had also remained the patron of Bulgaria in international relations. The Three Emperors' Alliance of 1881 had, as has been seen, provided for the eventual joining of Bulgaria and Eastern Rumelia. Despite strong efforts by the Russian government to establish good relations with Sofia, both the Bulgarian prince and his government refused to play the role of satellite. Friction soon developed between the Russian representatives in Bulgaria and the local officials, and between Alexander of Battenberg and the tsar. As a consequence by 1885 Russia had lost her controlling influence in the internal affairs of Bulgaria. Despite the change in the relationship with Russia, the Bulgarian national movement continued. The Bulgarians of Eastern Rumelia naturally wanted to join the Bulgarian state. In 1885 a revolt broke out in the Rumelian capital, Plovdiv. Alexander of Battenberg accepted the leadership of the movement and proclaimed the unification of the two areas.

Since the division of the large Bulgaria of San Stefano had been accomplished by international treaty, all of the great powers were involved in this action. The interests of the individual governments in the Bulgarian question, however, shifted. In 1878 Britain and Austria-Hungary had opposed the large Bulgaria because they had assumed that it would be a Russian puppet. Now that it was clear that Bulgaria was not under Russian tutelage and that the unification had been against Russian desires, Britain adopted another attitude toward the Bulgarian national goals. The Habsburg Empire, despite similar views, at this time remained loyal to the obligations of the Three Emperors' Alliance. The three states thus supported the maintenance of the provisions of the Treaty of Berlin and the blocking of the union. Alexander III was not against the unification in principle, but the action under these circumstances would have served chiefly to increase the prestige and popularity of Alexander of Battenberg and his government in Bulgaria.

At this point the Bulgarian cause was saved by the ill-advised actions of the Habsburg protegé Milan. The Serbian king's popularity within his own country had been gravely damaged by the tie with Vienna and his own inept rule. Since the union of Bulgaria and Eastern Rumelia had changed the balance of power between the two Balkan states, Milan felt obligated to seek compensation. Therefore in November 1885 he launched an attack on his neighbor. The action was a complete failure; the Bulgarian armies pushed into Serbia and the Habsburg government had to intervene to save its ally. Although Alexander of Battenberg gained no territorial rewards from his victory over the Serbs, the strength of the Bulgarian army, demonstrated in the war, showed the great powers that it would be difficult to undo the union. Alexander was thus recognized as prince of both provinces, but only for a five-year term. He thereafter ignored these provisions and proceeded with the real unification of the country.

Although it had suffered a diplomatic defeat on the issue of union, the Russian government continued to try to reestablish its influence in Sofia. In August 1886 a group of conspirators, with Russian foreknowledge, compelled Alexander to abdicate, and they took him out of the country. A new regime was set up, but it was soon overturned by a counterrevolution under the direction of Stefan Stambolov. Alexander was able to return to Bulgaria, but once back in the country he made the enormous error of telegraphing the tsar: "As Russia gave me my crown, I am prepared to give it back into the hands of its Sovereign." This statement not only offended the Bulgarians by implying the subordination of their nation, it gave Alexander III the opportunity of accepting the prince's offer to abdicate. A Regency was established, and once again Alexander of Battenberg was compelled to leave Bulgaria. Despite the departure of the prince, the Bulgarian government proceeded on its independent course. A new prince was now needed. After a long search, in July 1887 Ferdinand of Coburg was offered the position. This prince, of a German family, was an officer in the Habsburg army, and he obtained the permission of Francis Joseph before departing for Sofia.

With the election of a new ruler another period of intense international tension ensued. The Habsburg government had now reversed its position. The Three Emperors' Alliance had been based on the recognition of Habsburg predominance in Serbia and Russian control in Bulgaria. By 1887 Russian influence had been removed from Bulgaria, and with Habsburg approval. Russia, in fact, had been effectively excluded from the entire peninsula. The Bulgarian attitude of defiance had, of course, the strong support of Britain and the Ottoman Empire. These two powers and the Habsburg Empire now enjoyed the advantage that the principal gains made by Russia in 1878 had been annulled. The great question in international diplomacy was whether or not the Russian government would act and try to restore its former position by force.

The years 1886 and 1887 placed Bismarck in a difficult and dangerous position. Not only did Russia and Austria-Hungary clash over the Bulgarian question, in France General Boulanger, representing a policy of *revanche,* gained great popularity. Germany thus faced the diplomatic situation Bismarck had tried to avoid: France and Russia were both in a condition of crisis. It was by now clear that the Three Emperors' Alliance could not be continued. In 1887 neither Vienna nor St. Petersburg wished to participate in such a partnership. The agreement was therefore not renewed. To replace this pact Bismarck proceeded to construct another system of agreements. In June 1887 he made a bilateral pact with Russia, the Reinsurance Treaty. Here the two powers were guaranteed their partner's neutrality in case of an attack by a third power. Germany recognized Russia's preponderant position in Bulgaria and promised to oppose the restoration of Alexander of Battenberg. Russia's views on the Straits question were similarly accepted. At the time of the negotiation of this treaty Bismarck informed the Russian government of the contents of the Dual Alliance and made it clear that Germany would not allow the Habsburg Empire to be severely weakened or destroyed.

Having preserved the bonds between Berlin and St. Petersburg, Bismarck now turned to encouraging the formation of a countersystem to prevent Russia from taking action in the Balkans. In February, March, May and December, 1887, Austria-Hungary, Britain, Spain and Italy were joined in the Mediterranean Agreements, which were designed to assure the maintenance of the status quo in the Mediterranean and the Black Sea. These understandings were principally consultative agreements that did not bind the participants to any definite military action, but they did assure the cooperation of the signatories in diplomatic affairs.

For Austria-Hungary the most significant of the agreements reached at this time was the renewal of the Triple Alliance with changes that substantially altered the basis of the alignment. When the alliance had first been negotiated, Italy had clearly been the weakest of the three partners; she had not been in a position to dictate the terms of the treaty. In 1887 the Italian position was much stronger. The foreign minister, Count Carlo di Robilant, had been the ambassador in Vienna since 1871, and he was well acquainted with Balkan affairs. He was determined to use the Triple Alliance as an instrument to make gains for Italy in North Africa and in the eastern Mediterranean. He therefore wished to renew the agreement only on the condition that Italy obtain more favorable terms.

Because of the general European situation in 1886 and 1887, Bismarck was willing to make wide concessions. The Italian demands, however, involved Habsburg rather than German interests. Kalnoky was not in favor of allowing Italy a share in Balkan affairs, as Robilant now demanded. The Habsburg government wished to maintain this area as a field of negotiation with Russia, and perhaps Britain. Italian claims were also bound to infringe on the Habsburg preserve of the western half of the peninsula. The Habsburg minister was in the same manner not interested in supporting Italy's claims to African lands, because such a policy might bring his government into conflict with France over questions that did not involve Habsburg interests. In the final negotiations the monarchy was forced to concede in the Balkan field, but it did not become involved in the colonial question. The treaty of 1882 was renewed in the form in which it was originally drawn, but additional, separate provisions were annexed. In these Germany promised to support Italy against France, even should Rome take aggressive action as a result of events in Africa. In another section Austria-Hungary and Italy agreed to maintain the status quo in the Near East; if this should prove impossible, changes were to be made only after mutual consultation and on the basis of equal compensation for both powers. This compensation was not, however, to take the form of Italian acquisition of Habsburg territory. Italy was to receive no reciprocal gain should the empire annex Bosnia-Hercegovina.

In this renewal of the Triple Alliance Italy thus improved her position; the Habsburg Empire, in contrast, lost. The assurance given to Italy of an equal share in Balkan affairs was to cause great difficulties in the future. The Triple Alliance remained an advantage principally for Germany and Italy. In the next years the monarchs of these two countries exchanged visits and in 1888 a military convention was signed between them. In 1891 the alliance was renewed prematurely. It was now to last for twelve years unless one of the partners requested changes by 1896. The agreement was rewritten so that it formed a single document. Germany undertook further obligations toward Italy in regard to Africa, but the provisions binding upon Austria-Hungary remained unchanged.

The elaborate alliance system constructed by Bismarck in 1887—the Reinsurance Treaty, the Mediterranean Agreements and the renewed Triple Alliance—contributed to calming the international situation. The Bulgarian conflict with Russia remained, but the Russian government recognized that it could not intervene in that country. The following years were to witness even greater changes in the international scene. In 1888 William I died, to be succeeded by Frederick III, who lived but a short time, and then by William II. The new German emperor soon came into conflict with Bismarck and disapproved of many points of his policy. In 1890 when the Reinsurance Treaty came up for renewal, William II decided to drop it. He and other members of the German foreign office felt that it was in contradiction to the spirit of the Dual Alliance. They preferred an alliance system based on the cooperation of the Triple Alliance and Britain. Bismarck now left office, and the prime tenet of his policy, close relations between Berlin and St. Petersburg, was abandoned. The result he had so long feared soon came to pass. France and Russia, both diplomatically isolated, came together and in 1891 and 1894 signed military and political agreements. Europe was now divided into two camps, with France and Russia on one side and the powers of the Triple Alliance on the other. As long as Britain cooperated with the Triple Alliance the Habsburg government was a part of the stronger alignment.

Chapter 2

The Period of Equilibrium

The Ministry of Goluchowsky   Despite the changes in the alliance systems of the great powers, the 1890s were relatively calm on the continent. The main attention of the five states, Russia, Germany, Britain, France and Italy, was now directed primarily toward the colonial field and on the development of a "world" policy. The line of the alliances tended to blur and even to break down in the controversies that developed outside of Europe. Austria-Hungary alone among the major nations was not in a position to join in the contest for empire. Without adequate naval strength she could not hope to expand overseas. Internal difficulties and the general situation in southeast Europe prevented any moves on the European continent. The monarchy continued to play an important role in European diplomacy, but, like the other powers, she wished for a period of peace and calm in continental affairs.

The policy of moderation was well represented by the new foreign minister, Count Agenor von Goluchowsky, who came to office in May 1895. Polish in nationality, he held large estates in Galicia. Like the other Polish aristocrats of the empire, he felt no sympathy for Russia. He believed that Habsburg policy should be based on the Triple Alliance and cooperation with Britain. He wished to maintain what was

137

left of Ottoman control in the Balkans, and he opposed further Habs-
burg expansion in this direction. To him the occupation of Bosnia-
Hercegovina had been designed as a barrier against Slavic and
Russian influence and not as a bridge for a move southward toward
Salonika.

During the 1890s the powers were concerned with events in the
Ottoman Empire in regard to Armenia, Crete and Macedonia. Since
all of the states wished peace and feared a disturbance of the status
quo, they usually cooperated to calm matters down or to find a
solution by negotiation. The chief change in the political conditions
in the Balkans at this time concerned the island of Crete. In 1896
another Cretan revolt broke out, which led in 1897 to a war between
Greece and the Ottoman Empire. Although the Greeks were defeated, the powers intervened and forced the Porte to give the
island an autonomous regime with the Greek Prince George as governor. Thus for all practical purposes Crete became a part of
Greece.

During his ministry Goluchowsky had to deal with no major
crises similar to those of 1875–1878 and 1885–1887. This period did,
nevertheless, witness significant changes in the relationship of the
Habsburg Empire with Britain, Russia and Serbia. As has been
mentioned, Goluchowsky wished close relations with Britain. The
Mediterranean Agreements of 1887 had at least assured that Vienna
and London would consult in a crisis. These treaties had been made
by the British Conservative minister, Salisbury, and, according to
British constitutional practice, they were binding only on his cabinet. When in 1892 Gladstone returned to office, with Rosebery as
foreign secretary, the agreements were not recognized. After he was
reappointed in 1895 Salisbury wished to renew the relationship, and
he announced that he considered the treaties again in force. At this
time Britain was opposed by both France and Russia in the colonial
field and welcomed the cooperation of the Triple Alliance in the
Mediterranean and the Near East.

Since Austria-Hungary and Britain had the same aims, that is, the
preservation of peace and the status quo in the Balkans, cooperation
should have been easy to attain. Goluchowsky, however, wanted
more than the mere renewal and reaffirmation of the Mediterranean
Agreements. Extremely concerned with Russian penetration in the
Balkans, he wished to secure the assurance that Britain would fight
if Russia threatened to take the Straits or Constantinople. He feared

that once in control of the Ottoman capital Russia would be able to gain absolute predominance in the peninsula. Salisbury refused to accept additional obligations. He argued that the constitutional limitations on his power prevented him from concluding such an agreement. Britain still adhered to the policy of "splendid isolation," which forbade the making of general alliances. With the failure of the negotiations with Salisbury, Goluchowsky then turned to Russia to try to reach an understanding that would assure Habsburg security in the Balkans.

The failure of Austria-Hungary and Britain to renew the Mediterranean Agreements was to have strong repercussions in Italy, who had been a partner in the alignment but who had not been informed of the negotiations. The Italian government was naturally furious when it heard that the pacts, which it strongly supported, were no longer in existence. The Italians were also affected by the change in British policy that was now occurring. In 1882 Britain had occupied Egypt over strong French protests, and from that time on the British government began to shift the emphasis of its Mediterranean policy from the Straits to Egypt and the Red Sea. With the lessening of the British concern over the fate of Constantinople, the need for cooperation with Vienna was reduced. A policy of friendship with Italy, in contrast, was of value for Britain's Mediterranean interests.

With the dropping of the Mediterranean Agreements, Habsburg relations with Britain entered a period of decline. Thereafter the degree of friendship between London and Vienna was to be determined by the relations between Britain and Germany. The British government soon came to regard the Habsburg Monarchy as little more than a tool or satellite of the more powerful German empire.

Goluchowsky's decision to seek an agreement with Russia was welcomed in Berlin, where the German statesmen had every interest in preventing the recurrence of another Habsburg-Russian crisis in the Balkans. The Russian government, now deeply involved in the Far East, wished also to assure the tranquility of its western borders. The political situation in the Balkan peninsula had improved considerably for the Russians since 1887. Although the regime of Ferdinand of Coburg had at first been opposed by St. Petersburg, relations soon improved when the prince realized that Russian support was necessary should Bulgaria wish to further her territorial ambitions in Macedonia. In 1894 the anti-Russian premier Stambolov was dismissed, and in 1895 he was assassinated, much to the regret of Austria-Hungary. The accession of Nicholas II in 1894 also eased the friction between the states. In 1896 dipomatic relations were resumed.

In April 1897 Francis Joseph and Goluchowsky visited St. Petersburg. Here an agreement was made in which both powers agreed to refrain from adopting an active policy in the Balkans. They affirmed their desire to maintain the status quo; if changes became necessary they would consult and adopt a common policy. This understanding meant that for almost eleven years the Balkans remained outside the sphere of great-power conflict. In this period Macedonia became the chief center of unrest. The three neighboring states of Bulgaria, Serbia and Greece each tried to extend her influence into the area and win the population to her national cause. In 1903 a major revolt occurred against the Ottoman authorities. In accordance with their understanding of 1897 the Habsburg and Russian governments attempted to settle the issue between them, with only the limited participation of the other powers. In October 1903 Nicholas II, Francis Joseph, Goluchowsky and Russian foreign minister V. N. Lamsdorff met at Mürzsteg, where they drew up a reform program. As usual the effort did not succeed because of the failure of the Turkish government to implement the reforms. The policy of co-operation with the Habsburg Empire, illustrated by the Mürzsteg meeting, allowed Russia to enter the disastrous war with Japan with the assurance that Austria-Hungary would not use the opportunity to extend her influence in the Balkans. In 1904 the two powers made a further agreement, which gave Russia added security. They each pledged to maintain an attitude of neutrality should the other become involved in a war with a third power as long as the latter was not a Balkan state. The pact thus covered a Habsburg war with Italy, but not with Serbia, and, of course, the Russian conflict with Japan.

Although Habsburg-Russian relations improved, the friction between Rome and Vienna continued. Like the other great powers, Italy had embarked in the 1890s on an ambitious imperial program. In March 1896 the Italian armies suffered a crushing defeat at Adowa, and the plans for an Ethiopian empire collapsed. The government of Francesco Crispi was replaced by that of Antonio Rudini, who also supported a policy of loyalty to the Triple Alliance and cooperation with Britain. In 1891, when the Triple Alliance had been renewed, it had been agreed that the duration of the treaty would be twelve years unless one of the partners requested a change by 1896. The Italian government now asked that it be definitely stated in the pact that it was not directed against Britain. The German government refused, arguing that it would then appear as if the Triple Alliance were an anti-Russian alignment. Italian concern for British opinion remained strong. As will be shown, as British-German relations deteriorated, so did the ties of Italy with the Triple Alliance.

The greatest diplomatic reversal for Berlin and Vienna at this time was, however, the rapprochment between France and Italy carried out under the leadership of the Italian foreign minister, Emilio Visconti Venosta. Since Italy could do nothing about the French annexation of Tunis, it was now decided that it would be better to recognize the French conquest and to make some sort of arrangement to protect what Italian interests remained there. At the same time the French government, judging that Italy was the weak link in the Triple Alliance, determined that an effort should be made to detach this power from her alignment with Germany. The first step was the negotiation of a commercial treaty in 1898 that was favorable to Italy; the second was the French recognition of Italian claims to Tripoli, the last stretch of land not yet in European hands in North Africa. In an exchange of notes in December 1900 France recognized the Italian claims to Tripolitania and Cyrenaica in return for the Italian acceptance of the French position in Morocco. This agreement, however, did not signify an Italian desire to separate from the Triple Alliance. The Italian government simultaneously concluded a naval convention with Germany and Austria-Hungary providing for cooperation in the Mediterranean.

The Triple Alliance as revised, it will be remembered, obligated the Habsburg Empire to share with Italy control in Balkan affairs. The agreements with Russia in 1897 and again in 1903 were, nevertheless, based on the exclusion of other European powers, including Italy, from a deciding voice in the affairs of the region. In November 1897 Visconti Venosta and Goluchowsky met at Monza. Here the Habsburg minister told the Italian diplomat in only very general terms about the understanding with Russia. In these conversations the two foreign ministers adopted a common policy concerning the lands of the Ottoman Empire inhabited by Albanians. It was agreed that should the empire collapse a neutral and independent Albania would be established. This measure protected Habsburg and Italian exclusive interests on the Adriatic. Both powers opposed an extension of Serbian, Montenegrin or Greek control along the shores of the sea. No matter how strongly the two powers conflicted over the question of the domination of the Adriatic they were both determined not to allow a third state a share of influence in the area.

Despite this agreement, relations between Vienna and Rome deteriorated when in 1900 Victor Emmanuel III succeeded Humbert, who had been king since 1878 and had been sympathetic toward the Triple Alliance. Victor Emmanuel III was married to the daughter of Prince Nicholas of Montenegro, and a great effort was now made to increase Italian influence in that state. In 1901 Giuseppe Zanardelli, known as an irredentist, formed a cabinet with Giulio Prinetti as foreign minister. Prinetti favored a more active policy in Africa, the Balkans and the Mediterranean in general. He hoped to accomplish his aims through agreements with all of the powers. When the Triple Alliance came up for renewal in 1902, he requested that a statement be included that the agreement was purely defensive and not directed against France. He also pressed for a stronger recognition of the Italian claims in the Balkans and Africa. The German government again refused to consider further changes; the treaty was renewed in its original form.

In addition to the negotiations with the Triple Alliance partners Prinetti opened conversations with Britain and France. In 1902 the Italian government obtained British consent to its acquisition of Tripoli. In the same year, in an exchange of notes between Prinetti and the French ambassador in Rome, Camille Barrère, the Italian government undertook obligations to France that changed the entire character of the Triple Alliance. Here Italy agreed to remain neutral if France were attacked by one or two powers. In addition, and most significant, Italy promised her neutrality if France should declare war on Germany as the result of German provocation, as long as the Italian government was informed in advance and agreed that the conditions of the treaty had been fulfilled. Although it might be argued that the French-Italian accord was not against the letter of the Triple Alliance, it was certainly against its spirit. Neither Austria-Hungary nor Germany could henceforth be sure of the cooperation of Italy. The significance of the Italian rapprochement with France became even greater when in 1904 France and Britain joined in the Entente Cordiale and settled their colonial differences. The attraction upon Italy of this combination, with its predominant sea power in the Mediterranean, was extremely strong. The Moroccan crisis of 1905 showed the weakness of the Triple Alliance; Germany was deeply dissatisfied with the attitude of her Italian ally.

The relative passivity of Habsburg foreign policy during the ministry of Gołuchowsky reflected not only the general absence of diplomatic activity on the European continent but the increasingly difficult internal situation within the monarchy. From the beginning of the twentieth century it must be remembered that the Habsburg ministers in their conduct of foreign affairs were constantly hampered by the rapidly deteriorating conditions within the monarchy. The Ausgleich of 1867 had been arranged because no other alternative appeared possible at the time. Magyar nationalism was too strong a force to be resisted after the defeats in Germany and Italy. As has been mentioned, the state at this time was divided into two separate parts, with the Magyars dominant in one, the Germans in the other. The new arrangement, while solving some domestic problems, had led to a host of other complications.

Of the two sections, political conditions in Austria were certainly more in line with progressive political traditions. The Austrian constitution of December 1867 was to last until the collapse of the empire, but with changes made in the franchise. In 1907 universal manhood suffrage was introduced. After the Ausgleich the chief Austrian internal problem became the conflict of the Germans and Czechs in Bohemia. The Habsburg Empire had faced the challenge of German, Italian and Magyar nationalism in the past and had met defeat at the hands of each. Czech nationalism, based on growing national awareness and increasing economic power, now clashed with traditional German predominance. During the ministries of Eduard Taaffe (1879–1893) and Kasimir Badeni (1895–1897) attempts were made to find a solution, but little success was achieved. It should be noted, however, that Czech nationalism, unlike the movements previously discussed, did not at this time bring into question the integrity of the empire. No Czech groups of importance lived outside of the monarchy. Although there was some Panslav sympathy among Czech intellectuals, the Russian government did not give encouragement to political resistance within the empire. Russia had her Polish problem, and she also wished the maintenance of the empire.

Within the Austrian section two nationalities in addition to the South Slavs, who will be discussed below, continued to claim particular rights. The question of the Italians has already been described. They wished quite openly to join Italy through the cession of Trieste and the south Tyrol. In contrast, the Polish population remained a support to the empire. The Polish aristocrats of Galicia, in particular, were content with their position as long as the recreation of a free Poland was not possible. In their own province they dominated a minority—40 per cent—of Ruthenians. Quite obviously the condition of the Poles under Austrian rule was superior to that of those under the control of the Russians or the Prussians.

Although there was thus much national strife in Austria, the situation was much worse in Hungary. Here the Magyars, a bare majority in a population of 20,800,000 (1910 census), were determined to maintain their absolute predominance in their lands. The Hungarian Liberal party, representing the landowning aristocracy, followed a policy directed toward keeping both their own peasantry and the other nationalities in a condition of political subservience. Their general political aims within the empire were twofold. First, they attempted to Magyarize the non-Magyar population. They wanted the other nationalities to learn the Magyar language and to adopt Magyar culture and manners; they would thus be absorbed into the dominating nationality. Second, they tried constantly to gain increased privileges and influence in the empire as a whole. Their actions were to have a tremendous influence on foreign policy. Quite obviously the national question, involving the Rumanian and Slavic people of Hungary, caused a strong reaction on the other side of the borders. The policies within the empire were even more significant. The Magyar leaders, where possible, blocked reform in the entire monarchy. They did not wish changes in the Austrian section that would force similar alterations in their own policy toward the nationalities. They opposed in particular any action that would broaden the national base of the empire. They regarded the Ausgleich as the final solution to the Habsburg political problem, not as a step toward the establishment of a federal relationship in which all of the peoples would enjoy an influence proportionate to their numbers.

Although the Magyar statesmen fought change in the entire structure, they did seek alterations in the relations between Austria and Hungary that would increase their own independence. Their attacks on the common bonds with Austria centered on the army and the customs union. The extreme Magyar nationalists now wished the

Hungarian units of the Habsburg army to march together under
their own flag with Magyar as the language of command. The attack
on the army was met with great vigor by Francis Joseph. He regarded this sphere of state activity as his particular responsibility, and
he was not willing to see the military power of the empire so
weakened. By threatening to introduce universal suffrage into
Hungary, as he was to do in Austria, he was able to prevent the
army changes. In the economic field the Magyars were more successful. At every ten-year renewal of the customs union they fought
to extract more privileges and to emphasize their separate and independent position, even when such measures were detrimental to
their own interests.

Although these economic and military considerations were important, it was the Magyar attitude toward their minorities that was
to have the greatest effect on foreign policy. The negative influence
on Habsburg-Rumanian relations of the Magyar rule in Transylvania, where the Rumanians comprised 55 per cent of the population, has already been mentioned. The question of the Slavic people
was even more significant. The Hungarian state controlled a large
Slovak population but this group, which was only slowly arriving
at national self-consciousness, exerted relatively little influence in
Habsburg internal policy and almost none in foreign affairs. In contrast, the South Slavs—the Serbs, Croats and Slovenes—were soon
to become a major national problem, not only in the Hungarian, but
also in the Austrian, section of the state.

Within the monarchy the Croatian people lived primarily in the
Austrian province of Dalmatia and the Hungarian lands of Croatia
and Slavonia. The Slovenes were to be found entirely in Austria in
Carinthia, Carniola and Istria. The Serbs lived principally in the
Voivodina and in Slavonia, both parts of Hungary. Bosnia-Hercegovina was inhabited by both Serbs and Croats. In the years preceding World War I many political programs were developed that
aimed at giving the Slavic peoples of the empire a larger, preferably
an equal, share with the Germans and the Magyars in the control of
the government. The best known was the plan of Trialism, most
closely associated with the heir to the throne, Francis Ferdinand. In
this plan the Slavs would form a third component of the monarchy.

Whereas Trialism was based on reform within the empire, other
ideas clearly looked toward its disintegration. For instance, some
Croatian groups sponsored the concept of an independent Croatia.

However, for the foreign policy of the monarchy and the future of the state the most potentially dangerous was the Yugoslav idea. It was apparent that should the Croats, Serbs and Slovenes of the Habsburg Empire join with the Serbs of Serbia and Montenegro, a major state could be formed, equal at least to Italy in power status. This concept was attractive to the South Slav groups, who felt strongly their position of inferiority to the two dominant nationalities, particularly to the Magyars. The establishment of a Yugoslav state would quite obviously have meant the end of the Habsburg Monarchy as a great power and would have made virtually mandatory its division into its national components. As such it was a treasonable idea. Yet with the failure of the empire to move toward political reform in a national sense, the concept was bound to gain in popularity. Within the empire the political organizations of the South Slavs in both parts of the state came increasingly to adopt policies of cooperative action. In 1905 in the Fiume and Zara Resolutions the principal Serbian and Croatian political parties, now joined in the Serbo-Croat Coalition, agreed to work together to accomplish common political aims.

The Yugoslav question became a major issue in Habsburg foreign policy decisions after 1903, when events in Belgrade changed the political alignment of Serbia. From 1878 to 1903 Serbia had been under Habsburg influence, particularly during the reign of Milan Obrenović. In 1903 a revolt took place during which Alexander, Milan's son and successor, and his wife were assassinated and the rival Karadjordjević dynasty took control. Peter Karadjordjević, now king of Serbia, was to prove to be a ruler quite different from his predecessors. Although at first he concentrated on the consolidation of his power in the state, he showed himself very willing to lead a program of Serbian expansion. In this he worked closely with the Serbian Radical party and its leader, Nikola Pašić. The Serbian statesmen had two possibilities in developing the political power of their state. They could adopt a Greater Serbia program, looking forward to the gathering in of the Serbian lands under a centralized government, or they could espouse the wider Yugoslav idea, to be based on the concept of a federal South Slav state that would include Croats and Slovenes as well as Serbs. With either alternative Serbia could play the role of the Piedmont of the Balkans.

After 1903 Serbian relations with the monarchy were bound to deteriorate. The Serbian government looked upon Austria-Hungary as its chief opponent in foreign policy. The Habsburg statesmen consistently blocked Serbian attempts to move into Macedonia or toward the Adriatic; the monarchy controlled Bosnia and Hercegovina, which were the first objectives in any Serbian plan for national expansion. In addition, viewed from Belgrade the Habsburg Empire appeared a menace to the existence of Serbia. The extension of Habsburg control into Bosnia, Hercegovina and the Sanjak, together with the economic and political influences that were exerted in Montenegro and the Ottoman Macedonian and Albanian territories, all appeared moves designed to encircle and eventually crush the Serbian state. Like Piedmont before, Serbia felt strongly the need for the assistance of an outside power to strengthen her national position against the Habsburg Empire. She thus turned to St. Petersburg as a source of support. Russian aid could not be offered as long as the agreement of 1897 with Austria-Hungary held. Russian involvement in the Far East also made it imperative that no crisis errupt in the Balkans. It was only after the events of 1908 ended the cooperation of Russia and the Habsburg Empire that Serbia could hope for assistance from St. Petersburg.

As Serbia felt strongly menaced by Habsburg Balkan activities, the monarchy believed similarly that Serbia after 1903 constituted a grave danger to its internal security. In the past Austria-Hungary had consistently opposed the creation of any large Slavic state because such a power would limit Habsburg freedom of movement in southeastern Europe and might form a point of attraction for the Slavic peoples of the empire. The Serbia of King Peter, with its active national program, promised to be a much greater danger than a Greater Bulgaria could ever have been. Serbia certainly wished to expand her territories; the fortunes of the state were followed with deep involvement by many South Slav citizens of the monarchy. Under these circumstances the Habsburg government tried every means to combat the influence of Serbia both within the empire and in foreign relations. In Macedonia the Bulgarian and Albanian claims were favored against those of Serbia, and economic pressure was used when possible.

In the 1890s and in the first part of the twentieth century, as has been seen, the Eastern Question did not attract the major attention of the great powers, whose prime interests lay elsewhere. However, after 1907 the situation changed. In 1905 Russia not only met defeat in the Far East at the hands of Japan, but as a consequence of the

revolution of 1905 her internal political structure was changed. She
now joined the ranks of the constitutional monarchies. The setback
in the Far East and her internal problems led to a reassessment of
the Russian foreign policy position. In 1907 a colonial agreement
was signed with Britain in which the two countries settled their
differences in Central Asia, Tibet and Persia. With the closing of
the Far East and the Middle East as spheres of Russian activity, the
Ottoman Empire and the Balkan peninsula again became the center
of Russian attention.

Another change in the position of the powers in the Eastern Question had also occurred. As long as Bismarck was in office he carefully
refrained from involving Germany directly in Ottoman and Balkan
affairs. William II reversed this prudent policy. Close relations were
developed between Germany and the empire of Abdul Hamid II.
German experts played a major role in the Ottoman military reorganization and, like the other powers, Berlin obtained an important economic stake in the Ottoman Empire. The most significant
single enterprise undertaken under German sponsorship was the
Berlin to Bagdad railroad. Germany thus gained an interest in the
maintenance of the state that she had not had before.

The German position in the Near East by 1907 was influenced by
another important element. By this time the weight of the alliance
systems had gone against Germany. France, Britain and Russia were
joined in the Triple Entente. Italy was clearly an unreliable ally. The
Rumanian alliance had become weaker with the increasing efforts
at Magyarization in Transylvania. The French-German antagonism
had not abated, and, in addition, Germany through her competitive
naval and economic policies had come sharply into conflict with
Britain. The German government thus found that it had only one
reliable ally—Austria-Hungary. The nature of the relationship between Vienna and Berlin under these conditions began slowly to
change. In the time of Bismarck the German chancellor had taken
the leading role in determining the common policies of the two
states. Now the weight of influence shifted more to Vienna. The
German leaders could not afford to see their only friend suffer a
major setback in foreign policy, nor could they antagonize their ally
by failing to support her policies in the Balkans. Berlin therefore
gained an interest in Balkan developments quite as strong as that
of Vienna. In turn, the Habsburg Monarchy acquired the German
enemies. Although there were no outstanding differences at this

time between Vienna and the Western powers, the latter tended to regard the monarchy as little more than a satellite of Germany. Balkan developments were thus to be strongly influenced by the wider scheme of alliances that had developed over issues not related to Eastern affairs.

Chapter 3

From the Bosnian Crisis
to World War I

The Ministry of Aehrenthal   In 1906 Goluchowsky was replaced by
Count Alois Lexa von Aehrenthal, who was to become the last
Habsburg foreign minister to inaugurate an independent and active
policy. Like his two predecessors, he had been ambassador in St.
Petersburg. He strongly supported a policy of cooperation with
Russia, and in contrast to Goluchowsky he was willing to cede on
the Straits question. Strong-willed and ambitious, he wished Austria-
Hungary to act like a great power and not allow herself to be forced
into a position subordinate to either Germany or Russia.

In the same year Aehrenthal came to office, General Conrad von
Hötzendorff became chief of the Habsburg general staff. In subsequent years he was to exert great influence on foreign policy. A
close friend of Francis Ferdinand, he came to support the idea of
launching preventative wars against Italy and Serbia in the years
before 1914. His policies were opposed by both the foreign minister
and the aging Francis Joseph. Although the emperor still made the
final decisions in foreign policy, he was by 1906 seventy-six years
old. He had with time become increasingly adverse to inaugurating
new policies, and he tended to put off decisions. His influence thus
usually weighed on the side of moderation and the maintenance of
the status quo.

Aehrenthal's entire term as foreign minister was dominated by Balkan problems, in particular by the empire's relations with Serbia. By 1906 the two countries were already engaged in a bitter economic struggle. In 1904 Serbia had signed a treaty of friendship with Bulgaria. The agreement was to be the first step toward an eventual customs union. The Habsburg government saw this combination as the basis for a future large Slavic state and a hindrance to Habsburg influence in the Balkans. For this reason, and also from purely economic motives, the empire attempted to put pressure on Serbia to change her policies. In 1906 all livestock imports into the monarchy were prohibited. Since 80 per cent of the Serbian exports went to Austria-Hungary, and since the majority of the goods was livestock—pigs, cattle and poultry—this move was a blow to the Serbian economy. The prohibitions were favored by Hungarian agricultural interests, who did not like Serbian competition. This conflict, the so-called Pig War, was not settled until 1911. In fact, the Serbian economy ultimately benefited. New markets were found, and the Balkan state began to provide for its own food processing. More foreign investment was attracted into the country. With the general improvement in her economy, and with the increase of ties with the European countries, Serbia's need for an outlet on the Adriatic increased.

Desiring to inaugurate an active policy in southeastern Europe, Aehrenthal first attempted to provide for the construction of a railroad through the Sanjak to Mitrovica in Macedonia. Here it would link with the Turkish railroad to Salonika. The announcement of the plan caused a strong reaction from the other powers with interests in the Balkans. Russia protested that the action was in contradiction to the agreement that the status quo in the area would not be changed without consultation between St. Petersburg and Vienna. The Russian government now supported the Serbian desire for a railroad from the Danube to the Adriatic. In the end the Habsburg government abandoned the project, but the controversy it provoked should have given ample warning about the dangers of any Habsburg attempt to advance in the Balkans.

A much more serious situation arose almost immediately. In July 1908 the Young Turk revolution broke out in the Ottoman Empire; the new government announced the introduction of a constitutional regime. The status of both Bulgaria and Bosnia-Hercegovina came at once into question. According to the constitution, representatives from the Habsburg-occupied lands would sit in the Turkish parliament. The Habsburg government was deeply concerned about the new situation. It was well aware of the antagonism its administration had aroused in the provinces and the dangers in the apparently provisional character of its rule. It was felt that an annexation, with its appearance of permanency, would have a calming effect. Aehrenthal thus sought and received from his government approval of a change in the Habsburg position in Bosnia-Hercegovina. In a meeting of a crown council Conrad gave the opinion that action could safely be taken, as Russia was in no condition to go to war because of her recent defeat in the Far East and her internal condition. None of the Habsburg statesmen foresaw the strong reaction that the move was to cause among the other powers.

Since the Habsburg occupation had been approved in the Treaty of Berlin, a conference of the powers should have been held before the status of the provinces was altered. Aehrenthal, however, feared that other states, in particular Italy, would claim compensation if they were consulted too closely. He therefore preferred to come to an understanding only with Russia, in accordance with the policy adopted in 1897 and over the Macedonian problems in 1903. The Russian foreign minister, A. P. Izvolsky, was much like Aehrenthal. He wished to forward Russian interests and make gains in foreign policy. Unlike Goluchowsky, Aehrenthal was willing to make concessions on the Straits question so an agreement could be made on this basis. In September 1908 Isvolsky and Aehrenthal met at Buchlau in Moravia. Since no written record was kept, great disagreement exists on what actually took place at this time. It appears that Isvolsky agreed to the annexation of the provinces in return for a Habsburg promise to support the Russian position on the Straits. At this time the Russian government sought a new arrangement under which Russian warships could freely pass in and out of the Straits, but that the area would remain closed to the navies of other powers. The major point of disagreement was to come later over the question of timing. Aehrenthal claimed that he had informed the Russian minister that the annexation would precede the meeting of the delegations in October; Izvolsky maintained that it had been agreed that further consultations would be held before a move was made. After this meeting Izvolsky continued on to the Western capitals. He was on his way to Paris when the annexation was announced on October 6. On October 5, Ferdinand had declared the independence of Bulgaria. The two events, both in violation of the

Treaty of Berlin, caused an immediate crisis. Despite the Triple Alliance the Habsburg government had informed neither of its allies before the event, although they knew that an annexation was contemplated. William II, who learned of the Habsburg action on the day of its occurrence, was very angry. The annexation damaged German relations with the Ottoman Empire. The German chancellor, Bernhard von Bülow, however, argued that Germany had to support her ally: "To take a negative or even hesitant or grumbling position in the matter of annexation would never be forgiven us by Austria-Hungary."[14] The reaction of the entente powers, Britain, France and Russia, was highly unfavorable. The Turkish government immediately inaugurated a boycott of Habsburg goods. Izvolsky was, of course, placed in an impossible position. He was unable to obtain the needed Western support for the opening of the Straits for Russian warships, and it seemed as if he had completely betrayed Serbian interests in his agreement with Aehrenthal. Naturally he denied the Habsburg minister's version of the Buchlau meeting.

France, Britain and Russia now called for a conference to discuss the question. Aehrenthal refused to consider this proposal unless it was agreed beforehand that the annexation would be confirmed. The monarchy would obviously be outvoted in any such congress. Aehrenthal preferred to try to settle the matter through direct negotiations with the Porte, a move that was strongly supported by Germany. If the Ottoman government accepted the annexation there was little the other European powers could do. In February 1909 the Turkish government agreed to a settlement in return for a monetary compensation. Bulgarian independence was recognized in the same manner. At the time of the annexation the Habsburg government had announced that it intended to abandon its rights in the Sanjak of Novi Pazar. This action, which was probably a mistake, had been taken to block demands for compensation from Italy and to demonstrate to the powers that the empire did not intend to launch a policy of southward expansion. After Ottoman approval had been obtained, the principal problem remaining concerned Serbia.

The strongest protests against the Habsburg action had, as could be expected, come from Belgrade. The Serbian government had never lost the hope after 1878 that a situation would arise that would

---

[14] Oswald Henry Wedel, *Austro-German Diplomatic Relations, 1908–1914* (Stanford: Stanford University Press, 1932), p. 69.

allow it to take the provinces. The apparently provisional nature of the Habsburg rule had encouraged this idea. After the announcement of the annexation, Pašić had immediately consulted with the Russian government. A partial mobilization was also put into effect. The Serbs wished at the very least some form of compensation. The Habsburg government now responded in a very strong manner to the Serbian stand, insisting that Belgrade recognize the annexation and, in addition, change its attitude toward Austria-Hungary.

The Habsburg pressure on Serbia received the strong backing of Berlin. In March the German government delivered a note to St. Petersburg demanding that Russia accept the Austrian actions or Germany "would let matters take their course"[15]—that is, Germany would allow a Habsburg attack on Serbia. Faced with the demand, which was regarded as an ultimatum, the Russian government was forced to agree to the annexation. As Conrad had recognized, Russia could not risk war at this time. Serbia was advised to accept the Habsburg demands. The result of this diplomatic episode was thus an apparent victory of the powers of the Dual Alliance. Germany and Austria-Hungary together had triumphed over the other states of Europe. The action, however, destroyed the possibility of future Habsburg-Russian cooperation; the entente of 1897 was ended. From this time on the Russian leaders were determined to prevent further Habsburg advances. The backing that Berlin gave Vienna in this crisis marked the first time Germany had proved willing to support fully Habsburg special interests in the Balkans. It had now identified German aims with those of the Habsburg Empire.

The effect of the annexation crisis on Habsburg-Italian relations was also bad. In September 1908 Aehrenthal informed the Italian foreign minister, Tommaso Tittoni, that he intended to annex the provinces, but that he would at the same time abandon the Sanjak and give up the special rights that the empire held in Montenegro. The Italian minister was pleased at the surrender of these interests. When the annexation was actually announced, a great outcry came from the Italian public, which, of course, was not aware of the previous discussions. Irredentist claims were again loudly expressed. During this period Conrad advised a preventive war against both Italy and Serbia.

---

[15] Anderson, *The Eastern Question*, p. 285.

The Italian government disliked in particular the method used by Aehrenthal to carry through the annexation. Once again Russia and the Habsburg Empire had come together and had decided major Balkan questions to the exclusion of Italy. To prevent a recurrence of this situation Tittoni was determined to make his own arrangements with St. Petersburg. In October 1909 Nicholas II, Victor Emmanuel III and Tittoni met at Racconigi. Here they agreed on the maintenance of the status quo in the Balkans; if changes were to be made they were to follow the principle of nationality. The agreement was obviously directed against further expansion by the Habsburg Empire southward. The Russian and Italian governments also promised that they would enter into no special pacts on Balkan questions with a third party. Italy recognized the Russian position on the Straits; Russia supported the Italian claims in Tripoli.

Having made this secret agreement with Russia, the Italian government proceeded to conclude an apparently contradictory arrangement with Vienna. Here it was decided that if Austria-Hungary took the Sanjak, Italy would be entitled to compensation. Both powers also accepted the obligation not to make an agreement with a third power without informing the other partner. With these understandings with Russia and the Habsburg Empire, the Italian government believed that it had assured its position in the Balkans and had prepared the diplomatic background for a move in Africa.

From March 1910 to October 1914 Antonio di San Giuliano was the Italian foreign minister. Like his Austrian counterpart he believed in an active foreign policy, and he wished to use the Triple Alliance to further Italian aims. Since he did not trust Russia or the Slavic nations, he was in favor of the alignment with Vienna and Berlin. He feared that if the Habsburg Empire collapsed, Italy would have much more dangerous neighbors in the resurgent Slavic states. He was therefore more interested in making gains in the colonial field than in irredentism. In September 1911 the Italian government finally decided to take the North African lands for whose conquest such long preparations had been made. An ultimatum, designed to be rejected, was presented to the Ottoman government, and the war started.

From the beginning the campaign in North Africa went poorly. Because of the military failure here, the Italians were forced to use their naval power at the Straits and in the islands of the Mediterranean. This policy resulted in the temporary closing of the Straits and the strong opposition of the powers. Finally, in the Treaty of Ouchy in October 1912, Italy made peace with the Ottoman Empire and gained Tripoli. Throughout the conflict the Habsburg Empire did support Italy but insisted that the actual fighting be kept out of the Balkan peninsula and the Adriatic. At this time Conrad again urged his government to use the opportunity to go to war with Italy. In November 1911 he was dismissed from his post, but he was recalled in the next year.

Meanwhile, Aehrenthal had become ill, and he was forced to resign in February 1912. Although as foreign minister he had apparently made gains for the monarchy with the annexation of Bosnia and Hercegovina, he left the Habsburg international position in a condition worse than before he held office. Relations with Russia had deteriorated sharply; there was no longer a special relationship between the two states on Balkan matters. He had strongly antagonized Britain. The annexation in fact inaugurated a chain of events that led directly to the Balkan Wars and the eventual crisis of 1914.

The Ministry of Berchtold   Count Leopold Berchtold, who was Aehrenthal's choice as his successor, did not consider himself suited to the post. He preferred life on his estates to government affairs. Lacking his predecessor's energy and determination, he wished to inaugurate no new policies. In Balkan affairs he intended to maintain the Habsburg economic position, but he did not wish to acquire more territory. Since Serbia was clearly in the enemy camp, Berchtold now favored cooperation with Bulgaria. The basis of Habsburg policy remained the Triple Alliance, although Italy was pursuing an independent course.

The two Balkan wars of 1912 and 1913 were the main diplomatic events in Europe prior to the outbreak of World War I. After the Habsburg triumph in the Bosnian crisis it was the natural reaction of Serbia and Russia to unite to form a front against Austria-Hungary. The Russian representatives in Sofia and Belgrade were particularly active in this endeavor. Under their encouragement the Balkan states joined to form the Balkan League. After March 1912 a series of pacts were signed between Greece, Bulgaria, Montenegro and Serbia. Contrary to the Russian desire that this alignment be directed against the Habsburg Empire, its participants soon showed that they were far more interested in partitioning what remained of the Ottoman Empire in Europe than in furthering Russian diplomatic aims. The treaties provided for the division of the Turkish lands, with the Russian government given the position of mediator in case of disputes. Although the great powers did not know the exact details of these negotiations, they were aware that plans were being made. They all opposed a reopening of the Eastern Question at this time. On October 8, Russia and Austria-Hungary issued a joint warning, but the message arrived too late to prevent the outbreak of war. Thus Russia, who was instrumental in forming the alliance, saw it turn against her interests. The Russian government had no desire to see a further weakening of the Ottoman Empire. It also feared that the Bulgarian armies might enter Constantinople and occupy the Straits.

The Balkan armies were quickly victorious on all fronts. It was obvious that the Ottoman Empire would now lose its European possessions with the exception of the area around Constantinople. The successes of the Balkan states caused much concern in the Habsburg Empire. Great apprehension was felt over possible Serbian extensions of territory, particularly toward the Adriatic. Because of the joint interest of the Habsburg and Italian governments in preventing Serbia from becoming an Adriatic power, the two cooperated to secure the formation of an independent Albania. This policy had already been agreed upon in 1897 and 1900. Italy wanted to make the new state as large and independent as possible so that it could better resist Habsburg pressure.

A conference of the representatives of the powers meeting in London made the arrangements for the establishment of the Albanian state. The final organization was not settled by the outbreak of World War I, but a prince, William of Wied, was chosen. During the last phase of the Balkan Wars the Albanian lands continued to be the center of dispute. The chief crisis concerned the question of Scutari. This city had been assigned to Albania, but it was occupied by Montenegro. A great-power naval blockade and the threat of military action by Austria-Hungary forced Montenegro to withdraw. After the Second Balkan War an ultimatum from Vienna compelled Serbia similarly to surrender lands given to Albania.

While the great powers negotiated, the Balkan allies disputed the division of Macedonia. The formation of Albania meant that some lands that had been allotted to Serbia and Greece in the secret agreements were now to be a part of the new state. These nations therefore wanted to take Macedonian territories assigned to Bulgaria as compensation. Rumania, despite the fact that she had not participated in the war, similarly wished compensation, in particular the Bulgarian city of Silistria. Feeling herself surrounded by enemies, Bulgaria in June 1913 launched an attack on her former allies, who immediately combined against her. Rumania and the Ottoman Empire joined in this second Balkan war. The position of Bulgaria in this conflict became a matter of great concern to Vienna. The Habsburg policy was now the building up of this state as a check to Serbia. During the war the Habsburg government therefore attempted to secure support for intervention in the interest of Bulgaria. Neither Italy nor Germany would agree to this policy. The German government was more in favor of collaboration with Greece and Rumania. The king of Greece was the brother-in-law of William II; King Charles of Rumania was a Hohenzollern. The Second Balkan War ended in a severe defeat for Bulgaria. Serbia and Greece received the major share of Macedonia; Rumania took land in Dobrudja. Turkey kept Adrianople, which the Bulgarians had occupied. The defeated state, however, did obtain an outlet on the Aegean. In the settlement following the wars Serbia and Montenegro divided the Sanjak of Novi Pazar, giving these two Serbian states a common frontier.

After the Second Balkan War Habsburg relations with both Belgrade and Bucharest deteriorated further. The victory in the wars, as could be expected, resulted in a great upswing of Serbian national feeling. Within the state the impulsion for expansion gained in strength. For the Serbian patriot, as for his counterpart in the Italian, German and Hungarian national movements, the enemy was the Habsburg Empire. In the previous years various organizations had been formed whose aim was the active furtherance of the Serbian national cause. The most significant of these groups was the secret society called Union or Death, or the Black Hand. Founded in 1911, it numbered among its members many who were highly influential in Serbian political life, in particular Colonel Dragutin Dimitrijević, the head of intelligence of the Serbian general staff. The Serbian government watched the activities of these groups, but it was difficult to control them.

Animosity against the Habsburg government was also strong in another Balkan capital, Bucharest. The Rumanian government did not like the support that Vienna had given Bulgaria in the Second Balkan War. The question of Transylvania was becoming increasingly embittered. By 1914 it was recognized that in case of war Rumania could not be counted on as an ally despite the alliance that had been in effect since 1881. The strongest bond linking the country with Vienna and Berlin remained the king, with his strongly pro-German inclinations.

On the eve of World War I the Habsburg diplomatic position, despite these weaknesses and the changes that had occurred in the European alignments in the past years, was not entirely unfavorable. The Dual Alliance was the basis of Habsburg policy; Germany was the strongest military power of the time. Relations with Italy were not smooth, but the Triple Alliance had been renewed in December 1912. There was military and naval cooperation. The rivalry in the Balkans and the problem of the *irredenta* remained, but the two states had come together on the question of the establishment of Albania. The ties between Sofia and Vienna had been strengthened by the recent events. The Habsburg ally, Germany, had maintained good relations with Greece, Rumania and the Ottoman Empire.

The chief danger to the Habsburg position in eastern Europe and to its internal stability, in the opinion of the leading statesmen of the empire, continued to lie in Serbia and in the relation of that state to the South Slav movement within Austria-Hungary. As has been shown, after 1903 the Habsburg government had repeatedly clashed with the small state. Ultimatums had been delivered in connection with both the Bosnian crisis and the Albanian question. Although Conrad's advice that a preventive war be undertaken had not been followed, by 1914 it was generally agreed that another crisis might indeed have to be met in this manner. The occasion presented itself in June 1914. On the twenty-eighth of that month Francis Ferdinand and his wife were assassinated in Sarajevo, the capital of Bosnia. The deed was the work of the nationalistic Young Bosnian Society, which was aided by the Black Hand. The chief members of the plot had crossed over from Serbia; the weapon came from the Serbian state arsenal. It appears that Francis Ferdinand had been chosen as the target for the attack because of his political views. He had long opposed Magyar policy toward the other nationalities. Instead, he believed that the Slavic people should in some form be associated in the direction of the state on a basis of equality with the Germans and the Magyars. The revolutionary organization feared that when he came to the throne he would introduce such a plan and thus conciliate the South Slavs in the empire, who would then be averse to joining with Serbia in an independent state. In the previous May Pašić had learned that a plot was planned. He had tried to deliver a warning through the Habsburg minister of finance of the joint government, who was at the head of the administration of Bosnia-Hercegovina. Because the Serbian minister could not be explicit, he did not succeed in conveying his message. Francis Ferdinand had visited Bosnia against the strong advice of those who understood the unsettled conditions in the province. The security measures taken had also been inadequate.

After the assassination it was clear that the Habsburg government would have to take strong action. The citizens of the empire expected it. If an immediate move had been made against Serbia while the powers of Europe were still shocked by the act, the Habsburg government might have escaped precipitating a general war. Instead, it proceeded slowly. First the opinion of Germany was sought, then an investigation of the assassination was made. About a week after the event the monarchy asked its German ally what its attitude would be if war were declared on Serbia. At this time Germany agreed to back the Habsburg action. The German statesmen did not think Russia would fight on this issue; they also felt it necessary to support their ally. They could not afford to see Austria-Hungary fall, either from defeat by an outside power or from inner dissolution. The investigation of the assassination, undertaken at this time, failed to provide evidence of direct and official Serbian responsibility. The results therefore could not be used to justify action against Belgrade. Further delays were caused by the attitude of the prime minister of Hungary, Stephen Tisza. Representing the Magyar view, Tisza strongly opposed the launching of a war. He feared the reaction of Russia and Rumania, and he could not see what the empire could gain from such an action. He finally gave his consent on the condition that no Serbian territory be annexed after a victory.

With German support assured, and with the assent of the Magyar leader, the Habsburg government proceeded to formulate an ultimatum. During this period no attempt was made to consult either Germany or Italy on the text or the conditions. This method of procedure was adopted to prevent the Italian government from claiming compensation, but it did violate the terms of the Triple Alliance, which called for mutual consultation on Balkan affairs. At this time the Habsburg government knew that the Russian government was in consultation with Belgrade, but it was not clear whether or not Russia would go to war in support of Serbia. On July 23 an ultimatum with a time limit of forty-eight hours, which had been designed to be rejected, was delivered to Belgrade. Its most important demands were that the Serbian government give assurances that all activities directed against the Habsburg government on Serbian territory be stopped, that anti-Habsburg propaganda be suppressed and the national organizations be disbanded. Habsburg officials were to be allowed to participate in an investigation of the background of the assassination.

On July 25 the Serbian government returned a negative but conciliatory reply. It agreed to most of the terms of the ultimatum, but it rejected the participation of Habsburg officials, arguing that this action would violate Serbian sovereignty. Upon hearing of this reply William II believed that war had been avoided. The Habsburg government, however, was determined to act. The Serbian reply was rejected and diplomatic relations were immediately broken. Mobilization orders were issued and on July 28, again without consultation with its allies, the Habsburg government declared war on Serbia.

The next week was filled with feverish activity in all of the European capitals. The Habsburg action now brought the alliance systems into play. Both Germany and the Habsburg Empire hoped that the war would remain localized. The great question was the reaction of Russia. After much hesitation Nicholas II finally ordered partial and then, on July 30, full mobilization. This act brought the German military plans into operation. In the 1890s the Schlieffen Plan had been drawn up. Designed to meet the threat of a two-front war, its provisions took into account the expectation that Russian mobilization would take considerable time. If war broke out the German armies were first to attack and defeat France, and then only to turn against Russia. Since time was of the utmost importance to the success of the plan, the German government immediately after the Russian mobilization declared war on that power and subsequently on France. Britain entered the war against Germany on August 4. On August 6 Austria-Hungary went to war with Russia; the French and British declarations of war on the Habsburg Empire did not come until August 12. With these actions the major powers of Europe were all drawn into the second great conflict since 1815 to arise from the Eastern Question. This time the issue was not that of Russian domination of the Ottoman Empire but of the relationship between Austria-Hungary, Serbia and the South Slav problem.

Part IV

Conclusion: War and the Dissolution of the Empire

Chapter 1

World War I

With the outbreak of the war the major part of this narrative is concluded. The future would be determined more by military than by diplomatic decisions. The importance of military victory to diplomatic alignment was soon to be amply demonstrated. The Habsburg Empire had now entered upon the third major war arising from the national aims of its neighbors. The preceding two, although they involved European great powers, had not resulted in a general European war. In contrast, in 1914 the European alliance system drew almost the entire continent into the conflict. In the other wars the Habsburg Empire had fought alone; in 1914 it was allied with Germany. However, within this alliance it was clearly Berlin who held the dominating position. After the empire suffered military setbacks at the beginning of the fighting, this ascendency increased.

Once the war had started, the chief task of the foreign ministries of the belligerent states was to secure the support of the yet-uncommitted powers. For Germany and Austria-Hungary the attitude of Italy was of first importance. Because of the conditions through which the war had commenced, the obligations of the Triple Alliance did not bind Italy to enter. The pact was strictly defensive. During the period after the assassination the Italian foreign minister, San Giuliano, had maintained a passive attitude. Italy was not a strong military power, and it was important that no undue risks be taken. The Italian government also wanted to be in a position to demand compensation should the monarchy make gains at the expense of Serbia. When the text of the Habsburg ultimatum to Belgrade was received, the Italian government strongly attacked it and declared that the failure of Vienna to consult Rome was a violation of the Triple Alliance. Like the other weak powers, Italy maintained a passive attitude at the beginning of the war. Italian neutrality was declared and the military verdict awaited. In fact, the failure of Italy to join her allies at once signified that there was little chance that she would do so later. The question was rather whether she would remain neutral or ally with the Western powers. When it became clear that the central powers were not going to win a quick victory, the German government decided that concessions would have to be made to gain at least the neutrality of the state. In December 1914 the Italian government did take one positive action. After the beginning of the war the new Albanian government had disintegrated. Italy thus decided to occupy Valona to protect her Adriatic position and her interests in Albania. In the next years the Albanian territories fell under the control of the surrounding powers.

For the first year of the war Italy negotiated with both sides. At this time the German government strongly pressed the Habsburg Empire to make concessions, perhaps even to cede the south Tyrol. In January 1915 Berchtold was forced to resign over the Italian issue. He was replaced by Count Stefan Burian, who also stood firmly against giving in to the Italian demands. The three allied powers, France, Britain and Russia, were in a much better position to allow the Italian government the territories it desired. These now included the frontier of the Brenner Pass, possession of Istria, Dalmatia and the ports of Valona and Trieste. Italy expected, in addition, a share in any African or Middle Eastern lands taken by the other powers. Although the Western allies were willing to allow Italy any gains that could be made at the expense of the Habsburg Empire, Russia objected to the cession of Dalmatia, an act she regarded as a betrayal of Serbia. In the end the Treaty of London of April 1915, which brought Italy into the war, gave Rome only a portion of Dalmatia, but included almost all the other demands.

Although Italy was thus lost, the central powers won other allies. The eastern European states all followed the Italian pattern; they waited to see who would win and who would offer the highest reward for their participation. The first state to enter on either side once the conflict started was the Ottoman Empire. Here German influence was extremely strong; Russia was considered the main adversary. By November this power had joined Germany and Austria-Hungary. The next state to make a decision was Bulgaria, who came into the conflict almost a year later. Like the other powers the Bulgarian government first negotiated with both sides and awaited a clear indication from the battlefields. It was also concerned about the attitude of Rumania and Russia. The central powers were in a better position to bargain with Sofia since they could offer Macedonian territories that were in the possession of Serbia. In October 1915, after Germany had won great military victories over Russia, Bulgaria joined with the promise of Macedonia, some Serbian territories, and lands in the possession of Rumania and Greece should these powers enter on the side of the entente.

The Ottoman Empire and Bulgaria were to be the only states to support the central powers. In August 1916 Rumania entered on the side of the entente. In the negotiations the Rumanian government proved a very hard bargainer. Close relations were at this time maintained with Italy; the decision of Rome to join the entente made a deep impression in Bucharest. The Rumanian leaders were interested in Transylvania and Bukovina, which were under Habsburg control, and in Bessarabia, which belonged to Russia. They, like the Italians, would have preferred to have obtained a promise of a territorial reward in return only for neutrality. In the discussions with Rumania the German government again pressed the Habsburg Empire to make concessions, but the Magyars refused to bargain with Transylvania. Rumania thereafter joined the entente powers on the promise of Transylvania, Bukovina and the Banat. The Rumanian entrance was based on a grave miscalculation of German military strength. By December 1916 the German troops had occupied Bucharest; a peace treaty was signed in May 1918. In addition to Italy and Rumania, Greece joined the entente in July 1917, but only after an allied military intervention in the country.

Important as these events might be, the final decision of victory or defeat in the war was not to be determined in southeastern Europe. The major battles were waged in northern France and in east central Europe against Russia. During the course of the war the internal and the military situation of Austria-Hungary grew steadily worse. The first months of the war were a military disaster. Not only did the empire lose most of Galicia to the advancing Russian troops, the Serbian armies also defeated the Habsburg forces. In the spring of 1915 the German-Habsburg victory at Gorlice changed the picture for the moment. By the end of 1915 Serbia and Montenegro were taken. At the beginning of 1916 the general military situation appeared favorable to the central powers. Economic conditions, however, had deteriorated, and the empire as a whole depended strongly on German support.

As the war progressed and victory remained unattained, the national problem in the Habsburg Empire became progressively more difficult. The two considerations, military success and the retention of the loyalties of the national groups, were closely related. As had been demonstrated as early as 1848, a defeated empire would probably not survive. Although there was some sign of disloyalty in the army, most of the soldiers, no matter what their nationality, simply did their duty as citizens of the state. The Habsburg armies did not collapse until the final stage of the war. That they won no decisive victories, except in Italy, should cause no surprise. The Habsburg military forces were not particularly efficient; they had previously lost the only two wars in which they had engaged after 1815.

Despite the fact that the military authorities in the monarchy tended to regard the Slavic populations with distrust, there were no major signs of treasonable activity here either. The leaders of the national groups undoubtedly hoped to use the opportunity presented by the war to gain more special rights, but certainly the majority did not think of breaking up the empire. At the beginning of the war, nevertheless, some Czech and the South Slav political leaders did emigrate to western Europe. In November 1914 the Yugoslav Committee, composed of refugee Serb, Croat, and Slovene leaders, was formed. A similar organization under the direction of Thomas Masaryk was established for the Czechs. There were also Polish societies. These committees, which became significant only later in the war, gradually came to support more radical solutions. At first the British and French governments did not seek to exploit the national difficulties of the monarchy as a weapon in the war. They were mainly interested in the military defeat of Germany; Habsburg questions were secondary. The Russian government, in contrast, was always aware of the possibilities of the situation. In September 1914 Grand Duke Nicholas issued an appeal to the Habsburg minorities, assuring them of Russian support in the future. In the Western states the committees formed by the exiles were at first important mainly for their work of propaganda and for the influence their individual members won with the members of the French and British governments. They made considerable efforts to convince the entente statesmen that the empire was a prison for its people and that the majority of its inhabitants sought national independence.

The nationality problem was not only a disturbing element in internal Habsburg affairs, but also a point of conflict with Germany. The major question at issue with Berlin was the fate of the Polish lands, which had been conquered from Russia. As has been shown, the Polish aristocracy had consistently been a main support of the Habsburg government. Moreover, at this time the central powers needed Polish soldiers for their armies. They had every interest in conciliating Polish opinion. The Poles thus had to be given some assurance on their future political condition. Neither Germany nor Austria-Hungary wished to annex more Polish lands; they could not absorb a larger Polish population. Two alternatives remained. The Habsburg government favored the joining of Galicia to the Russian Polish lands to form a separate political unit, which would then be directly associated with the empire in some form. The Germans, in contrast, came to prefer the establishment of an independent Polish state that would be connected with Germany, or with both of the central powers, by close political and military ties. The Polish question remained in dispute throughout the war. No solution was ever found that was satisfying to the powers involved. The situation, in fact, became worse when in February 1918 the central powers made peace with the Ukraine. At this time, Germany wished to form a strong Ukrainian state as a balance to Russia, an action that directly affected the relations of the Habsburg Empire with its own Polish and Ruthenian subjects. In this treaty, lands that the Poles wished for themselves were incorporated into the Ukraine. It was not possible for the central powers to favor the Ukrainians without alienating the Poles. For the Habsburg Empire the assurance of Polish support was of far greater importance.

The military pattern of World War I, with the stalemate in the west and the German successes in the east, failed to provide the Habsburg Empire with the victory it so strongly needed. The monarchy lacked the resources and the internal stability to withstand a long and costly war. In 1916 Francis Joseph died. With him one of the foundations of the unity of the lands of the empire passed away. His successor, Emperor Charles, could not replace him either as a leader or as the symbol of the empire. From the beginning of his reign Charles recognized the urgent necessity of securing peace, and he sought every means to end the war. At the beginning of 1917, without informing his German ally or his foreign minister, Count Ottokar Czernin, he initiated discussions with the French and British governments through his brother-in-law, Sixtus of Parma. These negotiations fell through because of Italian insistence on the terms of the Treaty of London. In internal affairs he attempted to appease national discontent by summoning the Austrian parliament to meet in May 1917. These sessions, however, far from producing agreement, allowed the Czech and South Slav delegates to combine and attack the government.

The year 1917 brought great victories in the east for the central powers. By now Rumania was out of the war. At the end of the year Russia, who had undergone two revolutions, sought peace. In March 1918 the Treaty of Brest-Litovsk was signed. For their part the Western allies gained the adherence of the United States, who entered in April 1917. The defeat of Russia proved of little value to the empire. Although it was hoped that food supplies would arrive from the Ukraine and that the closing of the eastern front would ease the military situation, neither occurred. Great shortages now existed in both food and military supplies. The chaotic conditions in Russia allowed little hope of assistance from this area. Moreover, the communist victory had direct political effect upon the central powers. Socialist propaganda calling for a peace without victory made a deep impression throughout central Europe. In the first months of 1918 the Habsburg government had to deal with a series of strikes and mutinies that further hampered its efforts in the war.

The future of central Europe, however, still depended upon the fortunes of war. In the spring of 1918 the German armies launched their greatest offensive in western Europe. By the end of the summer it was clear that not only had this effort failed, but that the German military could not continue the conflict. From the middle of the summer of 1918 the collapse of the monarchy proceeded with great speed. The allies now recognized the national committees in exile. The Rumanian and Italian governments would, it was clear, take their national territories. The Serbs had come to terms with the leaders of the Habsburg South Slavs over the question of establishment of a Yugoslavia, although its exact form had not been determined. By September the Western allies had agreed to the formation of an independent Poland and a Czechoslovakia. In these last months of war the chief support of the Habsburg Empire, the army, finally collapsed. Its main force was concentrated in Italy. Here it not only lost battles but simply disintegrated. The soldiers deserted and made their way home.

With the dissolution of its army and the defeat of its German ally, the central government of the empire completely lost control of the situation. National administrations now took power in Prague and Zagreb. Revolutionary regimes were similarly set up in the capitals of the once predominant nationalities, Vienna and Budapest. On November 3 an armistice was signed; in the middle of the month Emperor Charles gave up his authority. At the same time separate republics of Austria and of Hungary were established. No trace of the former imperial structure remained.

The peace settlements imposed on the central European area after the war were in theory based on the self-determination of the peoples. Since it was impossible to draw boundaries that would cleanly separate the nationalities, all of the states that received territories from the former Habsburg Empire acquired at the same time minority groups. Thus in the postwar period the same conflicts that we have already seen within the monarchy continued in the new nations. The national struggle continued to play a major part in the internal life of all of the states and also in international relations. The basic problems raised previously concerning the interrelationship of the peoples of central and southeastern Europe were not solved by the altered political organization.

Although it is easy to criticize the settlements of 1919, it is difficult to suggest possible practical alternatives considering the conditions of the time. The Habsburg Empire had dissolved before the peace conferences were held. The monarchy, it must be remembered, was not only an association of nationalities; it also represented a political and social system that was under attack throughout Europe. The monarchs of the three conservative courts of Berlin, Vienna and St. Petersburg had always considered their fortunes bound together. This conviction had been the basis of the Holy Alliance and the Three Emperors' Alliance. In 1917 and 1918 they indeed all fell together. The new leadership in their countries sought the establishment of a radically different society. Within the lands of the Habsburg Monarchy few among the active, aggressive leaders considered a reconstructed empire desirable or possible after the final defeat; the national-liberal political ideal had triumphed everywhere.

Among the great powers the dissolution of the Habsburg Empire represented a contradiction in policies previously pursued. In the past all of the European governments had considered the continued existence of the monarchy a European necessity in order to maintain the balance of power. It was felt that, should the empire collapse, the Danubian and eventually the Balkan area would fall under the control of a single power, who could then from this base advance to the control of the continent. The empire was thus designed to be the "home" of the nationalities who were deemed too weak to survive alone. In establishing the new states and in strengthening the small powers who were already in existence (Rumania, Serbia and Greece), the Western allies, France in particular, considered that they would in cooperation be able to resist their larger neighbors. The other great multinational state of the continent, the Ottoman Empire, had already been deprived of its European possessions. Unfortunately, in subsequent years these governments were not able to protect their political independence. The dissolution of the Ottoman and Habsburg empires thus resulted in precisely the international situation the European statesmen in the nineteenth century had feared.

Chapter 2

Conclusion

Habsburg foreign policy in the years 1815 to 1918, as we have seen, had to deal primarily with the issues arising from the liberal and national movements and with the competing aims of Russia, France, Prussia, and, after 1870, Germany and Italy. In each of these contests the Habsburg government eventually lost. In an age when the other powers, even Italy, acquired large tracts of land in other parts of the world, the monarchy gained the little Republic of Cracow and impoverished Bosnia-Hercegovina, but simultaneously lost the rich provinces of Lombardy-Venetia and control in the Italian peninsula and the Germanies. In this period Habsburg territories and areas of influence were almost constantly the object of the policies of other states or national groups; in contrast, the main energies of the Habsburg government were usually concentrated on the attempt to maintain its empire intact, not to extend it. Thus, the Habsburg diplomats in general were engaged more often in responding to the initiatives of others than in inaugurating positive programs of their own. Much of this account has thus of necessity been directed toward a discussion of the policies of other governments, for instance, those of France, Prussia, Russia and Serbia, involving Austrian interests and possessions, instead of Habsburg moves against neighboring powers.

In addition to the setbacks in foreign affairs, increasing domestic strife at this time resulted in gradual internal disintegration and a sharp deterioration in the relations of the nationalities with one another. With this steady decline of power and prestige, the Habsburg Monarchy was in no condition to undergo a costly war or to withstand a complete defeat. Too much had been surrendered already. If the conflict of 1914 had been avoided, and if a long period of peace had been assured, perhaps another fate would have awaited the lands of the monarchy; but the circumstances of the defeat and the attitude of the victorious powers made the continuation of the empire almost impossible to contemplate.

In reviewing the course of Habsburg foreign policy in the century under discussion it is interesting to consider whether or not better leadership or the adoption of a different course in international relations could have averted the final catastrophe. The question is difficult to answer because of the enormous complexity of the issues involved. Certainly, the empire was directed by as competent a body of statesmen as led any other nation of the time; two, Metternich and Schwarzenberg, dominated their era. Francis Joseph, despite the many criticisms directed against him, was one of the most able of the European monarchs. The policies these men pursued were based in general on the hard realities of the Austrian position in Europe. After 1815 the Habsburg Empire could gain nothing by a policy of advancement. Like all territorially satiated states, the monarchy thus stood for the upholding of the status quo, for the sanctity of treaties and for legality in international relations. With only a few exceptions this program was maintained throughout the century. In foreign affairs the Holy Alliance in its varying forms represented this policy. In this alignment the monarchs of the three conservative courts stood together to protect their common political principles and to prevent changes in the map of Europe. As long as the alliance held, the Habsburg Empire was a part of a treaty system that could offer it protection and assistance in international relations. The alliance rested chiefly on the close and often affectionate association of the three rulers, and it served also to shore up the monarchical principle in European politics.

The weaknesses in the alignment have already been amply demonstrated. It functioned well only when Berlin and St. Petersburg were willing to forego an active foreign policy that clashed with Habsburg interests. The deep suspicion with which the Russian adventures in the Balkans were regarded in Vienna and the rivalry between the Habsburg and Prussian governments over primacy in Germany have been discussed. The alliance of the three courts broke down or was severely weakened four times in the century—during the Greek revolution, in the Crimean War, at the time of the Congress of Berlin and, finally, in 1887. In each case the principal cause for disaffection among the allies was Austria's refusal to sanction what appeared to be a dangerous advance of Russia power in the Balkans. The connection with Berlin, although troubled by frequent clashes over the German question, was maintained, except, of course, for the period of the Prussian unification of Germany. Despite its obvious drawbacks, the diplomatic combination of Prussia (Germany), Russia and the Habsburg Empire was the most advantageous alliance system for all of its participants.

The Habsburg Monarchy, in fact, had no other practical alternative; alliance with either of the other great powers, France or Britain, was not a real possibility. One of the most fascinating puzzles of nineteenth-century diplomacy is why the Habsburg Empire and Britain were unable to cooperate more effectively when they had so many interests in common, particularly in the Eastern Question. From the Austrian point of view collaboration with London was made difficult because Britain could do little to aid the empire in a time of crisis. The British navy could not defend a power with strictly continental problems. Another hindrance to British-Austrian friendship was that the British government in the affairs of western and central Europe tended to profess a great deal of at least vocal support for liberal-national movements, which were detrimental to Austria, despite its quite different stance in the Near East and the colonial world. Relations with France were on a similarly uneasy footing. Throughout this period France, even with conservative governments, appeared as the patron of revolutionary movements. The rivalry for control in Italy lasted until 1870; thereafter the intense French-German antagonisms effectively divided the two powers. German national feeling within Austria-Hungary made it improbable that the Habsburg government could consider an alignment with Paris against Berlin.

The great advantage of the alliance with Berlin and St. Petersburg lay in the fact that when it functioned it served to preserve the status quo. It can be asked here if perhaps that Austrian government would not have been wiser to have adopted a more flexible

policy toward changes in the European political organization and to
have at least tried to come to terms with the national movements
outside its boundaries. The attempt to guard the map of 1815 and to
prevent the formation of national states in the Balkans and in
central and southern Europe led to military defeat and severe setbacks in diplomacy. However, it is difficult, after a close study of the
events in each decade, to see how the empire could have reacted
in a different manner. The national movements in each case were
sponsored by a great power whose aim was also to increase its own
prestige and influence at the expense of Austria, as is shown in the
French role in the Italian unification, in the Russian position toward
the Balkan revolutionary movements and in the actions of Prussia
in the Germanies. Moreover, the national groups, both inside and
outside the empire, tended to be strongly antagonistic toward one
another. Thus the problem was not only that of the acceptance of
the national principle, but of finding a way to reconcile the conflicting aims and aspirations of the peoples. After the defeat by France
in 1859 and by Prussia in 1866, the empire did accept a unified Italy
and Germany; it simultaneously embarked upon a course of radical
change in its internal administration, with more attention given
thereafter to the nationality question. This alteration in policy
certainly did nothing to improve Habsburg fortunes. After 1870
the empire's position as a great power declined steadily.

Even with the advantage of hindsight it is virtually impossible to
see what other courses of action could have been followed that
would have more effectively contributed to the preservation of the
monarchy. The nineteenth century in European history marked the
victory of the national principle in the organization of states and in
international relations. The acceptance of this idea, if carried to its
logical conclusion, was bound to be destructive to a state based on
other concepts and composed of peoples whose prime loyalties were
increasingly being drawn away from the central government toward
their own national organizations.

The Habsburg Monarchy was the first great power in modern
times to suffer complete political annihilation. Poland, partitioned in
the eighteenth century, continued to exist as a national idea until
its reconstruction in 1918. It is now impossible to imagine a similar
resurrection of Austria-Hungary. A real "Habsburg" nationalism
does not exist. In a sense the dissolution of the state was part of a
development that has continued until the present day. World War I

not only resulted in the triumph of the nation-state in central Europe, it also inaugurated a process through which the European states lost their non-national territories either on the continent or overseas. After 1918 Russia was forced to surrender Finland, her Polish territories and, temporarily, the Baltic lands; Germany had her colonies taken from her. World War II contributed to the downfall of the British, French and Italian empires. Each of these states, based on a strong national core, continued as a great power. The Habsburg Empire, without a clearly predominating nationality, disappeared from the European state system.

Appendix

Habsburg Foreign Ministers, 1809–1918

Clemens Wenzel Lothar von Metternich   *October 8, 1809, to March 13, 1848*

Karl Ludwig Ficquelmont   *March 20 to May 4, 1848*

Johann von Wessenberg   *May 8 to November 21, 1848*

Felix zu Schwarzenberg   *November 21, 1848, to April 5, 1852*

Karl Ferdinand von Buol-Schauenstein   *April 11, 1852, to May 17, 1859*

Johann Bernhard von Rechberg   *May 17, 1859, to October 10, 1864*

Alexander von Mensdorff-Pouilly   *October 27, 1864, to October 30, 1866*

Frederick Ferdinand von Beust   *October 30, 1866, to November 8, 1871*

Julius Andrassy   *November 8, 1871, to October 8, 1879*

Heinrich von Haymerle   *October 8, 1879, to October 10, 1881*

Gustav Kalnoky   *November 20, 1881, to May 2, 1895*

Agenor von Goluchowsky   *May 16, 1895, to October 24, 1906*

Alois Lexa von Aehrenthal   *October 24, 1906, to February 17, 1912*

Leopold Berchtold   *February 17, 1912, to January 13, 1915*

Stefan Burian   *January 13, 1915, to July 22, 1916*

Ottokar Czernin   *July 22, 1916, to April 16, 1918*

Stefan Burian (second time)   *April 16 to October 24, 1918*

Julius Andrassy (the son)   *October 24 to November 2, 1918*

Ludwig von Flotow   *November 2, to November 11, 1918*

Suggested Reading

In this discussion of suggested further reading, the emphasis has been placed on books and articles dealing exclusively with Habsburg foreign policy. Only a few general works have been mentioned. There has thus been no attempt to cover such wide subjects as general European diplomatic history, the German and Italian unifications or the origins of World War I. Material on these subjects can be found in the bibliographies of the books listed below. This selection has been limited to works in English and a few titles in German.

The only book on Habsburg foreign relations in the period covered by this survey is R. Charmatz, *Geschichte des auswärtigen Politik Osterreichs im 19. Jahrhundert* (Leipzig: B. G. Teubner, 1919), 2 vols. The general history of the empire, including foreign policy, is discussed in Hugo Hantsch, *Die Geschichte Osterreichs* (Graz: Styria Verlag, 1962), Vol. II.; Hans Kohn, *The Habsburg Empire, 1804–1918* (Princeton: Van Nostrand, 1961); and A. J. P. Taylor, *The Habsburg Empire, 1809–1918* (London: Hamish Hamilton, 1948). The years between the Ausgleich and World War I are described in Arthur J. May, *The Hapsburg Monarchy, 1867–1914* (Cambridge: Harvard University Press, 1951). Habsburg relations with Britain are to be found in R. W. Seton-Watson, *Britain in Europe, 1789–1914* (Cambridge: Cambridge University Press, 1955) and with Russia in Barbara Jelavich, *A Century of Russian Policy* (Philadelphia: J. B. Lippincott, 1964). The Austrian involvement in the Eastern Question is included in M.S. Anderson, *The Eastern Question, 1774–1923* (London: MacMillan, 1966). The Habsburg position in international affairs is well presented in A.J.P. Taylor, *The Struggle for Mastery in Europe, 1848–1918* (Oxford: Clarendon Press, 1957). The nationality problem, so important for Habsburg international relations, is analyzed in the two books by Robert A. Kann, *The Multinational Empire: Nationalism and National Reform in the Habsburg Monarchy, 1848–1918* (New York: Columbia University Press, 1950), 2 vols; and *The Habsburg Empire: A Study in Integration and Disintegration* (New York: Praeger, 1957). The *Austrian History Yearbook*, vol. III, parts 1–3, is also devoted to this question.

The standard biography of Metternich is Heinrich Ritter von Srbik, *Metternich, der Staatsmann und der Mensch* (Munich: A. G. Bruckmann,

1925), 2 vols. Two shorter works in English are Helene du Coudray, *Metternich* (New Haven: Yale University Press, 1936); and Arthur Herman, *Metternich* (London: George Allen and Unwin, 1932). For the varying views on Metternich and his policy, the reader is advised to consult Henry F. Schwarz, *Metternich, the "Coachman of Europe": Statesman or Evil Genius?* (Boston: D. C. Heath and Company, 1962). Robert A. Kann, "Metternich: A Reappraisal of his Impact on International Relations," *Journal of Modern History*, XXXVII (December, 1960), 333–39, is similarly a discussion of the chancellor's general policies and their significance. There are two biographies of Metternich's associate, Friedrich Gentz: Golo Mann, *Secretary of Europe: The Life of Friedrich Gentz, Enemy of Napoleon* (New Haven: Yale University Press, 1946); and Paul R. Sweet, *Friedrich von Gentz* (Madison: University of Wisconsin Press, 1941). Metternich's career during the Napoleonic period is described in Enno E. Kraehe, *Metternich's German Policy: The Contest with Napoleon, 1799–1814* (Princeton: Princeton University Press, 1963); and his policies during the congresses of Troppau, Laibach and Verona in Paul W. Schroeder, *Metternich's Diplomacy at its Zenith, 1820–1823* (Austin: University of Texas Press, 1962) and "Austrian Policy at the Congresses of Tropau and Laibach," *Journal of Central European Affairs* (cited hereafter as *JCEA*), XXII (July, 1962), 139–52. The relation of the empire to the question of Greek independence can be found in Friedrich Engel-Janosi, "Austria and the Beginnings of the Kingdom of Greece," *JCEA*, I (April, 1941), 28–44, and I (July, 1941), 208–23.

There is still no standard biography of Francis Joseph equivalent to the Srbik study of Metternich. The best book in English is Joseph Redlich, *Emperor Francis Joseph of Austria* (New York: MacMillan, 1929). Egon C. C. Corti has written an extensive three-volume biography; its sections are entitled: *Vom Kind zum Kaiser, Mensch und Herrscher* and *Der alte Kaiser* (Graz: Styria Verlag, 1950–55). The best general discussion of the emperor's character is Heinrich Ritter von Srbik, "Franz Joseph. Charakter und Regierungsgrundsätze," in *Aus Osterreichs Vergangenheit* (Salzburg: Otto Muller Verlag, 1949), pp. 221–41. The life of Francis Joseph's first minister is described in Adolph Schwarzenberg,· *Prince Felix zu Schwarzenberg, Prime Minister of Austria, 1848–1852* (New York: Columbia University Press, 1946).

Austrian foreign policy during the Crimean War and in the period of Italian unification is covered in Charles W. Hallberg, *Franz Joseph and Napoleon III, 1852–1864* (New York: Bookman Associates, 1955); Franz Eckhart, *Die deutsche Frage und der Krimkrieg* (Berlin: Ost-Europa Verlag, 1931); Heinrich Friedjung, *Der Krimkrieg und die österreichische Politik* (Stuttgart and Berlin: J. G. Cotta'sche Buchhandlung, 1911); and in Paul W. Schroeder, "Bruck versus Buol: The Dispute over Austrian Eastern Policy, 1853–1855," *Journal of Modern History*, XL (June, 1968), 193–217. The events of the years 1856 to 1859 as viewed from Constantinople are to be found in Friedrich Engel-Janosi, "Once more: Three Years of the Oriental Question," *JCEA*, VII (April, 1947), 29–57. The Austrian involvement in the stages of the unification of Italy are given in Paul W. Schroeder, "Austria as an Obstacle to Italian Unification and Freedom," *Austrian History News Letter*, III (1962), 15–17; Howard McGaw Smyth, "Austria at the Crossroads: the Italian Crisis of June, 1848," in *Essays in the History of Modern Europe*, edited by Donald C. McKay (New York: Harper and Brothers, 1936), pp. 63–78; Franco Valsecchi, "European Diplomacy and the Expedition of the Thousand: The Conservative Powers," in *A Century of Conflict*, edited by Martin Gilbert (London: Hamish Hamilton, 1966), pp. 49–72; Nancy Nichols Barker, "Austria, France, and the Venetian Question, 1861–1866," *Journal of Modern History*, XXXVI (June, 1964), 145–54.

For the question of German unification the Austrian historian Heinrich Friedjung in his book *The Struggle for Supremacy in Germany* (London: MacMillan, 1935) includes the Habsburg point of view. The rivalry between Prussia and Austria in the Germanic Confederation is described in Enno E. Kraehe, "Austria and the Problem of Reform in the German Confederation, 1851–1863, *American Historical Review*, LVI (January, 1951), 276–94; and Friedrich Engel-Janosi, "Struggle for Austria in Berlin and Frankfort, 1849–1855," *JCEA*, II (April, 1942), 34–48, and Vol. III (July, 1942), 190–202. The diplomacy of Bismarck can be found in Chester W. Clark, *Franz Joseph and Bismarck: the Diplomacy of Austria before the War of 1866* (Cambridge: Harvard University Press, 1934). An analysis of Beust's policy after this war is in Hans A. Schmitt, "Count Beust and Germany, 1866–1870: Reconquest, Realignment or Resignation?", *Central European History*, I (March, 1968), 20–34. The Habsburg position before the Franco-Prussian War is discussed in Friedrich Engel-Janosi, "Austria in the Summer of 1870," *JCEA*, V (January, 1946), 335–53.

The diplomacy of the period between 1870 and 1914 has been the subject of many general studies and monographs. The majority, however, emphasize the policies of the other great powers. There are relatively few books that deal with Austria-Hungary alone. For the years after 1870 the first volume of Luigi Albertini, *The Origins of the War of 1914* (London: Oxford University Press, 1952–57), and Sidney Bradshaw Fay, *The Origins of the World War* (New York: Macmillan, 1939), should be consulted. The texts of the treaties in which the Habsburg Empire participated in these years are given in Alfred Francis Pribram, *The Secret Treaties of Austria-Hungary* (Cambridge: Harvard University Press,

1920–21). Volume two includes a discussion of the Triple Alliance. The years of this alignment and the Three Emperors' Alliance are covered in William L. Langer, *European Alliances and Alignments, 1871–1890* (New York: Alfred Knopf, 1950). Material on the Triple Alliance is also to be found in Fritz Fellner, *Der Dreibund* (Vienna: Verlag für Geschichte und Politik, 1960), and in the chapters on foreign relations in Christopher Seton-Watson, *Italy from Liberalism to Fascism, 1870–1925* (London: Methuen and Co., 1967). Hans Kohn, *Pan-Slavism: Its History and Ideology* (New York: Vintage Books, 1960), concerns the movement that was so important for Habsburg-Russian relations. The Balkan crisis of the 1870s is the subject of George Hoover Rupp, *A Wavering Friendship: Russia and Austria, 1876–1878* (Cambridge: Harvard University Press, 1941). A survey of Andrassy's career is given in Rowland Hegedüs, "The Foreign Policy of Count Julius Andrassy," *The Hungarian Quarterly*, III (1937), 627–42. Kalnoky is discussed in Friedrich Engel-Janosi, "The Resignation of Count Kalnoky as Foreign Minister of Austria-Hungary in May, 1895," *JCEA*, XI (October, 1951), 259–78. Goluchowsky's policies are to be found in Eurof Walters, "Goluchowsky and Aehrenthal," *The Contemporary Review*, CLXXVIII (October, 1950), 217–24; and J. A. S. Grenville, "Goluchowsky, Salisbury, and the Mediterranean Agreements, 1895–1897," *Slavonic and East European Review* (cited hereafter as *SEER*), XXXVI (June, 1958), 340–69. The relations of Italy and the empire before the war are given in William C. Askew, "The Austro-Italian Antagonism, 1896–1914," in *Power, Public Opinion and Diplomacy*, edited by Lillian P. Wallace and William C. Askew (Durham, North Carolina: Duke University Press, 1959), pp. 172–221.

The diplomacy of the years before the outbreak of the war is described in Alfred Francis Pribram's two books, *Austrian Foreign Policy, 1908–1918* (London: George Allen and Unwin, 1923) and *Austria-Hungary and Great Britain, 1908–1914* (London: Oxford University Press, 1951); and in Oswald Henry Wedel, *Austro-German Diplomatic Relations, 1908–1914* (Stanford: Stanford University Press, 1932). More detailed studies of events in this period are two articles by Salomon Wank, "Aehrenthal and the Sanjak of Novibazar Railway Project," *SEER*, XLII (June, 1964), 353–69, and "The Appointment of Count Berchtold as Austro-Hungarian Foreign Minister," *JCEA*, XXIII (July, 1962), 143–51; Margareta Faissler, "Austria-Hungary and the Disruption of the Balkan League," *SEER*, XIX (1939), 141–57; and Ernst C. Helmreich, "The Conflict between Germany and Austria over Balkan Policy, 1913–1914," in *Essays in the History of Modern Europe, op. cit.*, pp. 130–48.

The assassination of Francis Ferdinand and the beginning of World War I are the subjects of Vladimir Dedijer, *The Road to Sarajevo* (New York: Simon and Schuster, 1966), Joachim Remak, *Sarajevo, the Story of a Political Murder* (New York: Criterion Books, 1959), and of the second and third volumes of Luigi Albertini, *The Origins of the War of 1914, op. cit.* The war years and the dissolution of the empire are discussed in Arthur J. May, *The Passing of the Habsburg Monarchy, 1914–1918* (Philadelphia: University of Pennsylvania Press, 1966), 2 vols.; Z. A. B. Zeman, *The Break-Up of the Habsburg Empire, 1914–1918* (London: Oxford University Press, 1961); Harry Hanak, *Great Britain and Austria-Hungary during the First World War* (London: Oxford University Press, 1962); and Victor S. Mamatey, *The United States and East Central Europe, 1914–1918* (Princeton: Princeton University Press, 1957).

Index

Adbul Aziz, 116
Abdul Hamid II, 116, 148
Adrianople, Treaty of, 47
Aehrenthal, A. L. von, 150–56, 179
Aix-la-Chapelle, Congress of, 20, 26
Akkerman, Convention of, 46
Aksakov, I. S., 115
Albania, 112, 141, 142, 147, 157–59,
   166
Albrecht, Archduke, 85
Alexander I, 13, 15, 17, 19, 22, 23, 26,
   29–35, 41, 43–46, 78
Alexander II, 76, 111, 113, 116, 119,
   127
Alexander III, 115, 127, 132, 133
Alexander Obrenović, 146
Andrassy, J., 101, 102, 104, 106, 109–
   25, 127, 128, 179
Andrassy Note, 116
Augustenburg, Duke of, 95, 96
Ausgleich, 9, 101, 102, 104, 110, 125,
   143
Austroslavism, 58

Bach, A., von, 74
Bach System, 59, 89
Baden, 28, 29, 94
Badeni, K., 143
Balkan League, 156
Balkan Wars (1912, 1913), 156–59
Barrère, C., 142
Battenberg, Alexander of, 132–34
Batthyany, K., 64
Bavaria, 28, 29, 31, 47, 94
Belgium, 17, 36–38, 57, 97, 103, 104
Bem, Gen. J., 64
Berchtold, L., 156–62, 166, 179

Berlin, Congress of (or Treaty of),
   121–23, 125, 126, 128, 130, 132,
   152, 153, 175
Berlin Memorandum, 116
Bessarabia, 41, 76–78, 117, 118, 121,
   123, 130, 167
Beust, F. F. von, 100–4, 110, 111, 179
Biegeleben, L. von, 86, 96
Bismarck, O. von, 69, 79, 83, 84, 93–
   100, 102–4, 110–12, 116–18, 123–
   31, 134–36, 148
Black Hand (Union or Death) Society,
   158, 159
Bohemia, 4, 36, 59, 99, 143
Bosnia-Hercegovina, 113, 115–23, 125,
   127, 128, 135, 138, 145, 147, 151–
   54, 156, 159, 160, 173
Boulanger, Gen. G. E., 134
Brest-Litovsk, Treaty of, 170
Britain, 1, 2, 4, 5, 8, 13–15, 24, 26, 30,
   32, 33–35, 37, 40, 42–48, 50–53,
   60–66, 70–81, 83–89, 97, 104, 110,
   112, 113, 115, 116, 119, 121, 124,
   126–29, 132, 134, 136–42, 148,
   153, 156, 162, 166, 168, 169, 175,
   177
Bruck, K. L. von, 67
Bucharest, Treaty of, 41
Buchlau meeting (1908), 152, 153
Bukovina, 18, 41, 81, 167
Bulgaria, 112, 113, 115–22, 126, 127,
   131–34, 136, 139, 140, 147, 151–
   53, 156–59, 167
Bülow, B. von, 153
Buol-Schauenstein, K. F. von, 70–86,
   179
Burian, S., 166, 179
Burschenshaften, 29

185